Hiring with Authority

A Biblical and Governance-Based Framework for Church Hiring

Dr. Nathanael J. Lucas
Management Action Group LLC

Scripture quotations are from the King James Version (KJV) of the Holy Bible.

This book is intended solely for informational, educational, and organizational governance purposes. It does not constitute legal, tax, or employment advice. Churches and organizations are encouraged to consult qualified legal and financial professionals regarding employment law, compensation, and regulatory compliance.

The views expressed in this work reflect the author's theological convictions and professional experience. The principles described should be applied with prayer, discernment, and appropriate leadership oversight.

Any resemblance to actual people, organizations, or situations is coincidental, unless explicitly stated for illustrative purposes.

ISBN: 979-8-9945041-3-0

Printed in the United States of America

Published by:
Nathanael J. Lucas

In association with
Management Action Group LLC

Contents

Preface

This book exists to address a common, costly, and rarely acknowledged failure in church leadership. Churches hire with sincerity, prayer, and urgency, yet too often without governance. When this occurs, authority is delegated without clarity, values are affirmed but not enforced, and accountability is assumed rather than established.

Hiring in the church is not a staffing decision. It is a governing act. Every hire installs influence, models behavior, and grants authority that shapes doctrine, culture, and witness over time. When that authority is entrusted without discipline, the damage is rarely immediate but always cumulative.

This guide is written for pastors, elders, boards, and leadership teams who recognize that faithful hiring requires more than discernment and goodwill. It requires defined authority, values that govern behavior, and structures that protect both the church and those who serve within it.

This book assumes that an organization has identified its core values and understands its role as governing authority. Where values are undefined, unenforced, or treated solely as aspirational, the hiring authority cannot be exercised faithfully.

For readers seeking a disciplined approach to values definition and governance, **The LCSM10 Values Workbook** provides a structured foundation. While not required to read this book, values clarity is required to practice it well.

The chapters that follow are not designed to accelerate hiring. They are designed to restrain it. They exist to slow decisions, clarify authority, and protect the church from avoidable harm. Readers unwilling to govern hiring should not expect these principles to feel convenient. They are written to be faithful.

Part I
Why Church Hiring Must Be Governed

Church hiring is often treated as an administrative necessity rather than a governing responsibility. Positions are filled to meet immediate needs, relieve workload, or respond to growth pressures, with the assumption that spiritual sincerity or gifting will compensate for a lack of structure. This assumption has proven costly.

Every hiring decision places authority into the life of the church. Whether the role involves teaching, administration, counseling, worship, finance, or support, each hire instills influence, models behavior, and signals what is acceptable within the organization. People do not simply perform tasks. They shape culture, reinforce doctrine through action, and quietly define boundaries long before policies are ever enforced.

When hiring is ungoverned, authority becomes ambiguous. Expectations remain unclear. Accountability weakens. Correction feels personal rather than principled. Over time, churches drift, not because of open rebellion, but because no governing framework existed to protect alignment. Vision statements remain intact on paper while daily behavior moves in another direction.

Scripture treats the selection of leaders with seriousness and restraint. Biblical qualifications emphasize character before competence, faithfulness before giftedness, and order before expansion. These principles were not given to slow ministry, but to protect it. The early church understood that those placed in positions of responsibility would determine whether the body remained unified, credible, and faithful.

Governance does not replace prayer or spiritual discernment. It disciplines them. A governed hiring process provides clarity for leaders, protection for the congregation, and fairness for those being considered. It ensures that decisions are made consistently, not emotionally. It allows correction to occur without confusion and prevents crises that could have been avoided through patience and structure.

Before roles are defined, interviews are conducted, or offers are extended, the church must understand that hiring is an act of leadership governance with spiritual and organizational consequences.

The chapters that follow will address why hiring is never neutral, how values function as governing authority, and what is at stake when churches ignore these realities. Only after this foundation is established can a faithful, disciplined hiring process exist.

Chapter 1
Hiring Is Not Neutral

Every hiring decision a church makes alters its future. Whether the role appears spiritual or administrative, visible or behind the scenes, the act of hiring introduces influence, authority, and permission into the organization's life. Churches often underestimate this reality, assuming that good intentions, shared faith, or ministry passion are sufficient safeguards. They are not.

Hiring is never a neutral action. It installs a person who will shape behavior, interpret values, and reinforce culture through daily decisions. Long before sermons are preached or policies are referenced, staff members model what is acceptable, what is tolerated, and what is ignored. Over time, these signals become more influential than formal statements of belief or mission.

When a church hires without governance, authority becomes implicit rather than explicit. Expectations are assumed rather than defined. Correction feels relational instead of principled. Accountability becomes inconsistent. In such environments, conflict is personalized, and discipline is delayed or avoided altogether. The church may continue to function, but alignment quietly erodes.

Scripture consistently treats the selection of leaders as a weighty responsibility. The early church did not rush appointments nor prioritize convenience. Qualifications were public, observable, and tied to character and faithfulness. These standards were not designed to create elitism but to protect the body from instability and harm.

Modern churches often separate spiritual discernment from structural discipline, as though the two competed with one another. This separation creates vulnerability. Discernment without structure invites subjectivity. Structure without values becomes hollow. Faithful hiring requires both working together under authority.

This chapter establishes a critical truth that will govern everything that follows. Hiring does not merely fill a role. It grants influence. It communicates values. It determines whether the church will be led intentionally or drift under the weight of unexamined decisions. Recognizing that hiring is not neutral is the first step toward protecting the church through faithful, values-governed leadership.

Hiring as Delegated Authority

When a church hires an individual, it is not merely assigning tasks or filling a vacancy. It is formally delegating authority. This delegation may be limited or extensive, visible or behind the scenes, but it is real. Every employee acts, speaks, and decides within the authority granted by the church, whether explicitly defined or implicitly assumed.

Delegated authority allows an individual to represent the church in word and action. Staff members answer questions, resolve conflicts, manage resources, teach, counsel, and make daily decisions that shape how others experience the church. Even roles considered administrative carry authority because they influence access, communication, priorities, and response. Authority is present whenever discretion is given.

Problems arise when churches confuse delegation with assistance. Help can be temporary. Authority is enduring until it is clearly limited, supervised, or withdrawn. When authority is delegated without definition, individuals fill the gaps with personal judgment, preferences, and assumptions. Over time, this becomes the church's functional culture, regardless of stated beliefs or policies.

Scripture assumes that authority must be entrusted carefully. Leadership in the church is always exercised on behalf of others and under accountability. Delegation does not remove responsibility from those who grant it. Elders, boards, and senior leaders remain accountable for the authority they extend, even when misuse or failure occurs at lower levels.

Hiring as delegated authority requires clarity. Roles must specify not only responsibilities, but also limits. Decision rights must be understood. Lines of accountability must be visible. Without this structure, correction becomes difficult, and discipline feels arbitrary. With it, leadership can act decisively, fairly, and redemptively.

Understanding hiring as delegated authority changes how churches approach the entire process. It slows decisions, raises standards, and demands alignment before placement. It also protects those being hired by giving them clear expectations and defined boundaries. Delegated authority, when governed by values and exercised with accountability, becomes a stabilizing force rather than a hidden risk.

This reality reinforces the chapter's central truth. Hiring is not neutral because it installs authority. Recognizing and governing that delegation is essential to faithful church leadership.

Why Staffing Decisions Shape Doctrine, Culture, and Witness

Staffing decisions determine who is permitted to teach, model behavior, interpret values, and represent the church in daily life. While doctrine may be articulated from the pulpit and written into statements of belief, it is reinforced or weakened through the actions, speech, and priorities of those placed in authority. Over time, what is practiced consistently carries more influence than what is proclaimed occasionally.

Doctrine is shaped not only by formal teaching but by informal reinforcement. Staff members answer questions, offer counsel, lead prayer, and make judgment calls that communicate theological assumptions. When individuals lack doctrinal alignment or clarity, they introduce confusion through tone, emphasis, and omission rather than overt contradiction. Small deviations, left unaddressed, gradually redefine what the church actually believes.

Culture is formed through repeated behaviors that are permitted, rewarded, or ignored. Staffing decisions instill those behaviors. A church's culture is not created by slogans or vision statements. It emerges from how leaders respond to conflict, handle correction, speak about others, and make decisions under pressure. Staff members model these responses daily, teaching the congregation what is acceptable without ever stating it directly.

Witness is shaped by consistency between belief and behavior. Those who represent the church in public interactions, pastoral care, administration, and community engagement become the visible expression of its faith. When staffing decisions are made without regard for character, maturity, or alignment, credibility suffers. The church's message is weakened when conduct does not match its confession.

Because staffing decisions simultaneously shape doctrine, culture, and witness, they must be governed with care. Churches cannot separate employment from leadership influence. Every hire communicates values, sets boundaries, and establishes patterns that will either strengthen or erode faithfulness over time.

Recognizing this reality forces a shift in perspective. Staffing is not about filling positions. It is about stewarding influence. The health of the church depends not only on what it teaches, but on whom it entrusts with authority to live it out before others.

Consequences of Ungoverned Hiring

When hiring decisions are made without clear authority, defined values, and enforceable structure, the effects are rarely immediate. Ungoverned hiring does not usually result in instant failure. It produces gradual erosion. Over time, this erosion weakens leadership clarity, organizational stability, and spiritual credibility.

One consequence of ungoverned hiring is doctrinal drift. This drift is often subtle. It appears in tone, emphasis, and omission rather than open contradiction. Staff members interpret Scripture, counsel congregants, and respond to questions through their own theological framework when alignment has not been clearly established. Without governance, these interpretations become normalized, even when they quietly diverge from the church's stated beliefs.

Another consequence is cultural inconsistency. When values are not defined and enforced through hiring, behavior becomes personality-driven. Some actions are corrected while others are ignored. Standards vary depending on who is involved or how much conflict leaders wish to avoid. This inconsistency creates confusion and resentment, both among staff and within the congregation.

Ungoverned hiring also weakens accountability. Correction becomes difficult because expectations were never clearly stated. Leaders hesitate to address issues for fear of appearing unfair or unloving. Over time, unresolved problems accumulate, and small issues harden into patterns that are costly to address. Discipline, when it finally occurs, feels abrupt and personal rather than principled and redemptive.

Relational strain is another outcome. Staff members hired without clarity often experience frustration, burnout, or defensiveness. They may feel blindsided by expectations that were never articulated or resentful of boundaries that were never explained. These tensions damage trust and unity, making collaboration increasingly difficult.

Finally, ungoverned hiring harms the church's witness. When internal confusion becomes visible through public conflict, moral failure, or leadership instability, credibility suffers. The congregation and surrounding community lose confidence in leadership, not because of a single decision, but because the absence of governance allowed problems to grow unchecked.

The consequences of ungoverned hiring serve as a warning. Good intentions do not replace structure. Spiritual language does not eliminate the need for clarity. Faithful churches protect doctrine, culture, and witness by governing hiring decisions with patience, discipline, and values-based authority.

Chapter 2
Values as the Governing Authority

Values are not aspirations. They are governing convictions that establish boundaries, define behavior, and authorize enforcement. In the life of the church, values answer a foundational question before vision, strategy, or staffing are ever considered. They determine what is permitted, what is corrected, and what is protected when pressure arises.

Many churches confuse values with culture statements or inspirational language. When values are treated this way, they lose authority. They become descriptive rather than directive. In practice, this means decisions are driven by personalities, urgency, or perceived effectiveness rather than by conviction. Hiring becomes reactive instead of governed.

Governing values function as a form of authority that precedes leadership discretion. They are not adjusted to fit people. People are evaluated against them. When values are clearly defined and consistently enforced, they remove ambiguity from decision-making. Leaders are no longer required to rely on intuition or relational leverage to correct behavior. The standard already exists.

In hiring, values determine who may be entrusted with influence. They shape role definitions, interview questions, and evaluation criteria long before resumes are reviewed. Without values acting as governing authority, churches default to visible competencies, emotional chemistry, or perceived gifting. These may appear spiritual, but they are insufficient to protect doctrine, culture, and witness.

Scripture consistently places values, expressed through character and faithfulness, above ability and performance. This priority is not accidental. Ability can amplify both faithfulness and error. Values determine which one will be amplified. When values are clear, hiring decisions become acts of stewardship rather than acts of convenience.

Until values are understood as governing authority, churches will continue to hire based on outcomes they hope for rather than convictions they are willing to enforce. Faithful hiring begins when values are elevated from statements to standards and from language to authority.

Values Versus Personality, Gifting, And Charisma

Personality, gifting, and charisma are often mistaken for indicators of readiness or suitability for church leadership. They are visible, persuasive, and easy to affirm. Values, by contrast, are quieter. They reveal themselves over time through consistency, restraint, and obedience, especially under pressure. Because of this difference, churches frequently elevate what is immediately impressivc over what is ultimately governing.

Personality influences style. Gifting affects effectiveness. Charisma draws attention. None of these qualities determines faithfulness. A compelling personality may mask immaturity. A strong gift may amplify poor judgment. Charisma can inspire confidence without producing integrity. When hiring decisions are shaped primarily by these traits, authority is granted without adequate protection.

Values function differently. They govern behavior when no one is watching. They determine how authority is exercised, how conflict is handled, and how Scripture is applied in difficult situations. Values reveal what an individual will protect, compromise, or confront when outcomes are uncertain or unpopular. These realities cannot be assessed solely by performance.

Scripture consistently warns against elevating appearance, ability, or outward success above character. Leadership qualifications emphasize self-control, faithfulness, humility, and household integrity, not presence or persuasiveness. These are values-based measures. They exist to protect the church from being led by competence without conviction.

Gifting and charisma are not to be dismissed. They have their place within the body. The problem arises when they are treated as substitutes for values rather than as expressions governed by them. When values are unclear or unenforced, personality becomes the default authority. When values are clear, personality becomes a servant rather than a driver.

Faithful hiring requires restraint. It requires leaders to look beyond what is immediately effective and evaluate what will be consistently faithful. Values must govern the use of gifting and charisma, not the other way around. Only then can authority be entrusted without risking the church.

Why Vision And Mission Fail Without Values Governance

Vision and mission statements articulate direction and purpose, but they do not govern behavior on their own. Without values functioning as enforceable authority, vision becomes aspirational language, and mission becomes an activity-driven effort. Both may sound compelling, yet neither possesses the power to restrain, correct, or protect when pressure is applied.

Vision describes where a church intends to go. Mission explains what it exists to do. Values determine how that journey is undertaken and what boundaries may not be crossed along the way. When values are undefined or unenforced, vision and mission are interpreted subjectively. Each leader applies them according to personal preference, temperament, or perceived urgency. Over time, alignment fragments.

Many churches attempt to address misalignment by revising their vision or expanding their mission language. This approach fails because the underlying problem is not direction or purpose. It is authority. Vision and mission do not possess enforcement power.

Values do. Without values governance, leaders lack a shared standard for decision making, correction, and discipline.

In hiring, this failure becomes visible quickly. Candidates may verbally affirm the church's vision and mission while operating from a different set of convictions. Without values acting as a governing authority, there is no mechanism to evaluate alignment beyond stated agreement. Once authority is delegated, discrepancies emerge through behavior rather than belief statements, and correction becomes difficult.

Values governance provides the missing structure. Values establish non-negotiables that protect vision from compromise and mission from drift. They clarify what success looks like beyond outcomes and define what will be upheld even when growth, popularity, or convenience are at stake.

When values are governed, vision gains stability and mission gains integrity. Leaders are no longer forced to choose between faithfulness and effectiveness. Hiring decisions, strategic choices, and corrective actions can be made with consistency and confidence. Without values governance, vision and mission may inspire, but they will not endure.

How values function as boundaries, not aspirations

Values are often presented as ideals to strive toward rather than standards to be upheld. When values are treated as aspirations, they describe what a church hopes to become someday. When values function as boundaries, they define what a church will and will not permit today. This distinction determines whether values have authority or merely sentiment.

Aspirational values invite interpretation. They inspire discussion but resist enforcement. Boundary-based values establish limits. They clarify behavior, decision-making, and accountability. In governed organizations, values are not negotiated under pressure. They are already settled and serve as the reference point for action.

Boundaries protect both people and purpose. They make expectations visible and consistent. When values operate as boundaries, leaders do not need to invent corrective language or rely on personal authority to address misalignment. The value itself provides the standard. Correction becomes principled rather than relational, and discipline becomes restorative rather than punitive.

In hiring, this distinction is critical. Aspirational values allow nearly anyone to appear aligned. Boundary-based values require evidence. They demand demonstrated patterns of faithfulness, restraint, and integrity. Candidates are evaluated not on their enthusiasm for the values, but on their willingness to live within them.

Scripture consistently treats godly standards as boundaries. Commands, qualifications, and warnings exist to protect the people of God from harm and confusion. They are not suggestions. They establish order and responsibility. When churches dilute values into aspirations, they unintentionally remove the very structure Scripture provides for leadership and care.

Values that function as boundaries create stability. They define what is protected when outcomes are uncertain and what must be corrected when behavior drifts. Without boundaries, values lose authority. With them, values become a governing force that sustains faithfulness over time.

Chapter 3
The Cost of Getting It Wrong

The cost of poor hiring decisions in the church is rarely immediate, but it is always cumulative. Ungoverned hiring does not usually lead to an instant collapse. It produces gradual damage that compounds over time, often remaining unnoticed until the consequences are difficult or impossible to reverse. Churches pay this cost not only through organizational instability but through spiritual harm, broken trust, and diminished witness.

When authority is placed into roles without clear values and governance, doctrine becomes vulnerable. Teaching may remain technically sound while application drifts. Counsel becomes inconsistent. Scripture is filtered through personal conviction rather than shared belief. Over time, the church no longer knows what it stands for, only what it tolerates. This drift is not caused by open rebellion, but by quiet misalignment left uncorrected.

Cultural damage follows closely behind doctrinal erosion. Behavior becomes personality-driven rather than principle-driven. Standards fluctuate depending on who is involved, how effective they appear, or how costly correction might be. Faithfulness becomes secondary to performance. Those who operate within clear boundaries feel frustrated, while those who test limits learn that enforcement is inconsistent. Trust erodes, and unity weakens.

The human cost is often the most painful. Staff members hired without clarity experience confusion, burnout, or resentment. Expectations shift without explanation. Correction feels personal instead of principled. Leaders delay difficult conversations, hoping issues will resolve themselves. When action is finally taken, it feels abrupt and damaging, even when necessary. Relationships suffer because governance was absent at the beginning.

The public witness of the church also bears the weight of ungoverned hiring. Moral failure, leadership conflict, or abrupt staff departures do not remain internal. Congregations feel disoriented. Communities become skeptical. The church's message is questioned not because the gospel has changed, but because leadership appears unstable or untrustworthy.

Financial and strategic consequences often follow. Resources are redirected from the ministry to crisis management. Momentum is lost and vision stalls. Churches find themselves repairing damage instead of advancing mission. In many cases, these outcomes were not inevitable. They were the result of decisions made too quickly, standards left undefined, or values left unenforced.

This chapter is not written to assign blame or inspire fear. It exists to restore seriousness to a responsibility often minimized. Hiring decisions carry weight because they install authority. When values govern that authority, the church is protected. When it is not, the cost is paid slowly, repeatedly, and publicly.

Spiritual Harm

Spiritual harm is the most serious and least visible cost of ungoverned hiring. It rarely announces itself through dramatic failure. More often, it develops quietly through confusion, inconsistency, and diminished spiritual authority. When individuals are placed in roles of influence without values governance, the spiritual health of the church gradually weakens.

Authority in the church carries spiritual weight. Those who teach, counsel, lead prayer, or model faith are shaping how Scripture is understood and lived. When alignment is unclear, mixed messages emerge. Scripture may be handled sincerely but inconsistently. Conviction becomes optional. Obedience is softened. Over time, the congregation learns not from doctrine alone, but from what is permitted and ignored.

Ungoverned hiring also affects spiritual trust. When leaders operate without shared convictions or accountability, congregants sense instability. Counsel differs from person to person. Correction feels uneven. Discipline appears selective or absent. This inconsistency causes people to question whether spiritual authority is grounded in truth or convenience.

Another form of spiritual harm occurs when gifting is elevated above maturity. Highly capable individuals may be placed in leadership roles before they are spiritually prepared to bear the weight of influence. Without values-based boundaries, pressure exposes weaknesses rather than producing growth. Instead of being discipled, individuals are positioned prematurely, and both they and those they lead suffer as a result.

Spiritual harm also manifests through silence. Leaders hesitate to confront error or sin for fear of conflict, loss, or public discomfort. Over time, what is unaddressed becomes normalized. The church may retain the language of faith while losing its clarity of conviction. The result is not overt rebellion, but gradual accommodation.

The cost of spiritual harm is difficult to measure, but its effects are lasting. Confusion replaces confidence. Conviction yields to preference. Faith becomes performative rather than formative. These outcomes are not the result of bad theology alone, but of authority entrusted without governance.

Protecting the spiritual health of the church requires more than sincerity and prayer. It requires discipline. Hiring decisions must be governed by values that prioritize faithfulness, maturity, and accountability. Without this protection, spiritual harm accumulates quietly, shaping a church that no longer reflects the truth it proclaims.

Organizational Instability

Organizational instability is a predictable outcome of ungoverned hiring. When authority is placed in roles without clearly defined values, responsibilities, and accountability, the church's structure becomes fragile. Decisions are made inconsistently, expectations shift without explanation, and leadership operates reactively rather than intentionally.

Instability often begins with unclear roles. Staff members are hired to meet immediate needs, but boundaries are not established. Authority overlaps or remains undefined. Individuals make decisions based on personal judgment rather than shared standards. Over time, confusion increases as leaders respond differently to similar situations. What was once manageable becomes chaotic.

Leadership turnover is another indicator of instability. Staff hired without clarity often experience frustration or burnout. They may feel unsupported, misunderstood, or unfairly corrected. When departures occur suddenly or frequently, the organization loses continuity. Trust erodes among remaining staff and volunteers, who become uncertain about expectations and leadership direction.

Ungoverned hiring also disrupts decision-making processes. Without values acting as a governing authority, leaders rely on urgency, relational pressure, or perceived effectiveness. Long-term planning gives way to short-term problem-solving. Strategy becomes fragmented as each leader prioritizes what they consider most important.

Instability affects volunteers and congregants as well. Inconsistent leadership creates confusion about vision, priorities, and standards. Volunteers hesitate to commit when leadership direction appears uncertain. Ministries struggle to sustain momentum because leadership support fluctuates.

The cumulative effect of organizational instability is exhaustion. Leaders spend increasing amounts of time managing conflict, clarifying misunderstandings, and repairing relationships. Energy that should be devoted to ministry and discipleship is redirected toward maintaining basic functionality.

Organizational stability is not the result of control or rigidity. It is the product of a governed authority. When hiring decisions are grounded in clearly defined values and enforced consistently, roles are clarified, leadership is aligned, and the church operates with confidence. Without governance, instability becomes the default, and the cost is paid repeatedly over time.

Moral Failure And Public Scandal

Moral failure and public scandal are among the most visible and devastating consequences of ungoverned hiring. While these events often appear sudden, they are rarely isolated or accidental. In most cases, they emerge from patterns of compromised standards, unclear accountability, and authority granted without sufficient governance.

When values are not enforced as governing authority, boundaries become flexible. Behavior that should prompt correction is minimized, explained away, or ignored, especially when the individual involved is effective, well-liked, or perceived as indispensable. Over time, private compromises grow bolder, and restraint weakens. What was once unthinkable becomes rationalized.

Ungoverned hiring frequently places individuals into positions of influence before their character has been tested under pressure. Gifting, charisma, or public success may mask unresolved issues of integrity, pride, or self-control. Without clear values and accountability structures, there is little resistance when temptation arises. Authority becomes a shield rather than a responsibility.

Public scandal rarely stems from a single decision. It results from prolonged silence, delayed correction, and an unwillingness to confront behavior that threatens the church's witness. Leaders may fear conflict, reputational damage, or division, leading them to overlook warning signs. By the time action is taken, the damage is already public.

The consequences of moral failure extend far beyond the individual involved. Congregations experience disillusionment and grief. Trust in leadership is fractured. The surrounding community questions the church's credibility. Even when repentance occurs, restoration is complex and often misunderstood, particularly when governance was absent from the beginning.

Scripture treats moral qualification as foundational for leadership, not optional. These standards exist to protect both the leader and those under their care. When churches ignore or dilute them, they do not become more gracious. They become more vulnerable.

Preventing moral failure and public scandal requires more than reactive discipline. It requires governed hiring that prioritizes character, enforces boundaries, and establishes accountability before authority is entrusted. When values are clearly defined and consistently applied, the church is better protected, and leadership is exercised with humility and restraint rather than risk and exposure.

Long-Term Damage To Trust

Trust is built slowly and lost quietly. In the church, trust is not sustained by charisma, growth, or public success. It is sustained by consistency, integrity, and faithfulness over time. Ungoverned hiring undermines this foundation by introducing instability, inconsistency, and unresolved tension into leadership structures.

When authority is granted without clear values governance, congregants begin to sense unpredictability. Decisions appear inconsistent. Standards seem to change depending on the person involved. Correction is applied unevenly or avoided altogether. Over time, people stop assuming that leadership actions are guided by conviction and begin to suspect they are driven by convenience or favoritism.

Trust erodes further when problems are handled quietly but not clearly. Staff departures occur without explanation. Roles change suddenly. Ministries are reorganized without transparency. Congregants may not know the details, but they recognize patterns. When leadership does not communicate clearly or act consistently, people fill the gaps with suspicion rather than confidence.

Ungoverned hiring also damages trust within leadership teams. Staff members become cautious in their relationships, uncertain about expectations or boundaries. Collaboration weakens as individuals protect themselves rather than serve openly. When trust is low, honesty feels risky, and alignment becomes performative rather than genuine.

The most damaging effect of lost trust is disengagement. Volunteers withdraw. Giving becomes cautious. Attendance may continue, but investment decreases. People remain physically present while emotionally distant. Once trust is broken, it is difficult to restore, even after leadership changes or corrective action is taken.

Trust cannot be demanded or repaired through messaging alone. It is rebuilt through consistent, principled action over time. Governed hiring protects trust by ensuring that authority is entrusted carefully, standards are enforced fairly, and decisions are made transparently. When values guide hiring, trust has a foundation. Without them, trust becomes fragile, and the damage lasts long after the original decision is forgotten.

Early Discernment Questions for Values-Governed Hiring

The following questions are not designed to evaluate competence or performance. They are intended to reveal how a candidate understands authority, accountability, and faithfulness. These questions should be used early in the hiring process, before roles are finalized or authority is extended.

- Tell us about a time when you were corrected by leadership. How did you respond, and what did you learn from it?
- When effectiveness and faithfulness appear to be in tension, how do you decide which takes priority?
- Describe a situation where you disagreed with leadership direction. How did you handle that disagreement?
- What boundaries do you believe are necessary for those serving in church leadership?
- How do you respond when leadership expectations limit your gifting or abilities?
- In your view, what disqualifies someone from leadership, even if they are effective?
- How should a church respond when a leader's behavior contradicts its stated values?
- What does accountability look like when it is exercised faithfully and biblically?

These questions are not meant to produce perfect answers. They are meant to reveal patterns of thought, posture toward authority, and alignment with governed values. The responses should be evaluated collectively, prayerfully, and with patience.

Part II

Establishing Hiring Authority Before the Search

Most hiring failures in the church do not begin with the wrong candidate. They begin with unclear authority. Before a position is posted, resumes are reviewed, or interviews are scheduled, the church must determine who has the right to hire, what authority is being delegated, and under what values that authority will operate. Without this foundation, even well-intentioned searches produce confusion and conflict.

Hiring authority is often assumed rather than defined. Pastors believe they can hire because they lead. Boards believe they can hire because they govern. Ministry leaders believe they can hire because they are overwhelmed. When these assumptions are not clarified, responsibility becomes fragmented. Decisions are made informally, accountability is blurred, and correction becomes difficult once authority has already been granted.

Establishing hiring authority is not about control. It is about stewardship. Authority must be assigned deliberately and exercised consistently. This requires clarity regarding who approves roles, who conducts interviews, who makes final decisions, and who bears responsibility when outcomes fall short. When authority is clear, leaders are protected, and candidates are treated fairly.

Values governance must be established before the search begins. Values define the boundaries within which authority operates. Without them, hiring criteria are shaped by urgency, availability, or perceived effectiveness rather than conviction. Establishing values governance early prevents pressure from redefining mid-process standards.

This section focuses on the decisions that must be made before engaging candidates. It addresses how hiring authority is assigned, how roles are defined under authority, and how governance protects both the church and those it seeks to employ. Faithful hiring does not start with interviews. It starts with clarity.

The chapters that follow will provide structure for defining authority, writing enforceable roles, and establishing alignment before authority is ever delegated. Churches that govern hiring before the search are better prepared to protect doctrine, culture, and witness through disciplined leadership decisions.

Chapter 4
Who Has the Right to Hire

Before a church considers whom to hire, it must determine who has the authority to make that decision. Hiring authority is not self-evident, nor do title, tenure, or workload automatically grant it. When the right to hire is unclear, responsibility becomes fragmented, and accountability is weakened before the process even begins.

In many churches, the authority to hire is assumed rather than established. Pastors may assume authority because they lead spiritually. Boards may assume authority because they govern organizationally. Ministry leaders may assume authority because they feel the pressure of unmet needs. When these assumptions coexist without clarity, hiring decisions are made inconsistently, often informally, and sometimes in conflict with one another.

The right to hire must be explicitly assigned. This assignment should reflect the scope of authority being delegated and the level of influence the role will carry. Positions that involve teaching, counseling, discipline, financial stewardship, or public representation of the church require a higher level of oversight than support roles with limited discretion. The greater the authority granted, the greater the governance required.

Scripture consistently links authority with accountability. Those who appoint leaders are responsible for the authority they extend. Delegation does not remove responsibility from elders, boards, or senior leaders. It distributes it. When hiring authority is delegated without clear oversight, failures are often blamed on individuals rather than on the leaders who authorized the placement.

Clear hiring authority protects everyone involved. It prevents power struggles among leaders. It ensures candidates are evaluated consistently. It allows correction to occur without confusion or defensiveness. Most importantly, it anchors hiring decisions to shared values rather than personal preference or urgency.

Determining who has the right to hire also requires distinguishing between recommendation and decision. Many voices may provide input, discernment, and counsel. Few should hold final authority. When this distinction is not honored, responsibility is diluted, and governance collapses under the pressure of consensus.

Faithful churches establish hiring authority before the search begins. They define who approves the role, who conducts the process, who makes the final decision, and who remains accountable for the outcome. Hiring authority, once clarified and governed, becomes a stabilizing force that protects the church from confusion and drift.

Before authority is delegated to a candidate, authority must first be clarified among those who lead.

Elders, Boards, Pastors, And Delegated Authority

Hiring authority in the church must reflect the structure of leadership and governance already in place. Elders, boards, pastors, and delegated leaders each carry different forms of authority, and confusion among these roles often leads to misaligned, contested, or poorly governed hiring decisions. Clarity is not optional. It is foundational.

Elders bear spiritual oversight. Their authority is rooted in doctrine, shepherding, and the protection of the flock. When a role involves teaching, spiritual formation, counseling, or discipline, elder involvement is not merely appropriate; it is necessary. Even when elders do not conduct interviews or manage staff directly, they retain responsibility for the authority exercised in their name.

Boards typically carry fiduciary and organizational governance authority. They are responsible for legal compliance, financial stewardship, and structural integrity. When hiring decisions involve compensation, contractual obligations, risk exposure, or organizational structure, board oversight is required. This does not mean boards manage ministry, but it does mean they must govern the conditions under which authority is granted.

Pastors often operate at the intersection of spiritual leadership and daily operations. In many churches, pastors are given practical hiring authority because they lead staff, set direction, and bear responsibility for execution. This authority, however, must be defined and bounded. Pastoral authority to hire is not absolute. It operates within the governance established by elders and boards and must remain accountable to shared values and oversight.

Delegated authority exists when hiring responsibility is assigned to ministry leaders, department heads, or executive staff. Delegation is appropriate and often necessary, but it does not transfer ultimate accountability. Those who delegate hiring authority remain responsible for the outcomes. Delegated authority must be limited, supervised, and clearly defined, especially when the roles being filled carry influence beyond a narrow scope.

Problems arise when these authorities overlap without clarity or are exercised independently without coordination. Elders may assume pastors are handling alignment. Boards may assume elders are addressing spiritual qualification. Pastors may assume delegated leaders are operating within values. In reality, no one is governing the whole.

Faithful hiring requires alignment among these authorities. Each must understand its role, its limits, and its responsibility. Elders protect doctrine and spiritual integrity. Boards protect structure and stewardship. Pastors lead execution and supervision. Delegated leaders operate within clearly defined boundaries.

When these roles are aligned and governed by shared values, hiring decisions become disciplined rather than reactive. Authority is extended carefully, accountability remains intact, and the church is protected from confusion and drift before the first interview ever occurs.

When Staff Hires Become Governance Decisions

Not every hire in a church carries the same weight, but every hire carries some level of authority. The distinction that matters is not whether a position is labeled "staff" or "leadership," but whether the role exercises influence, discretion, or representation on behalf of the church. When it does, the new hire moves from an operational matter into a governance decision.

Staff hires become governance decisions when they involve teaching Scripture, shaping belief, counseling others, handling discipline, managing finances, or representing the church publicly. These roles do more than perform tasks. They interpret values, model behavior, and exercise judgment. Authority is present wherever discretion exists, regardless of job title.

Churches often reserve governance language for senior leadership roles while treating other staff positions as purely administrative. This distinction is misleading. Administrative roles can control access, communication, scheduling, information flow, and resource allocation. These functions influence culture and decision-making in subtle yet powerful ways. When such roles are filled without governance, authority is exercised without accountability.

Another indicator that a staff hire has become a governance decision is longevity. Temporary or seasonal roles may carry limited authority, but long-term placements embed influence into the organization. Over time, these individuals shape norms, expectations, and informal rules. The longer the tenure, the greater the need for values governance at the point of hiring.

Staff hires also become governance decisions when they operate with minimal supervision. Independence increases authority. When leaders assume alignment without structure, correction becomes difficult, and trust is strained. Governance at the hiring stage provides clarity before independence is granted.

Recognizing when staff hires become governance decisions changes how churches approach the process. It elevates standards, slows timelines, and requires broader oversight. It also protects staff members by providing clear expectations and accountability from the beginning.

Faithful churches do not wait for problems to redefine authority. They recognize governance decisions early and treat them with appropriate seriousness. When staff hires are governed, authority is stewarded rather than assumed, and the church is protected from unintended consequences that emerge long after the hire is made.

Role Clarity And Approval Thresholds

Role clarity is a governance requirement, not an administrative preference. Before a church considers candidates, it must define the role with enough precision that authority, responsibility, and accountability are unmistakable. When roles are vague, authority expands informally, expectations shift over time, and justification for correction becomes difficult. Ungoverned roles inevitably produce ungoverned behavior.

Clear roles answer three foundational questions. What authority is being granted? What responsibilities are expected? What accountability mechanisms will govern the role? If any of these elements are unclear, the role cannot be faithfully staffed. Hiring into ambiguity transfers confusion from leadership to individuals and embeds it in the organization.

Approval thresholds exist to match oversight with authority. Not every role requires the same level of approval, but every role requires the appropriate level. Positions with limited scope, short duration, and close supervision may be approved at a lower level of leadership. Roles that teach, influence culture, manage resources, or represent the church publicly require greater approval and broader governance involvement.

When approval thresholds are undefined, churches default to convenience. Leaders hire quickly to relieve pressure, often without realizing they have exceeded their authority. Later, when problems arise, responsibility is disputed. Elders may claim they were not consulted. Boards may claim they were unaware. Pastors may claim they assumed alignment. The absence of thresholds creates shared confusion and fractured accountability.

Approval thresholds also protect candidates. Clear governance ensures that individuals are not placed into roles without proper authorization or support. It prevents situations where a hire is later questioned, undermined, or reversed because authority was unclear. Faithful governance provides stability for both the church and the individual serving within it.

Establishing role clarity and approval thresholds before the search begins disciplines the hiring process. It slows decisions appropriately, raises questions early, and ensures that authority is extended deliberately. When roles are clearly defined, and approval thresholds are honored, hiring becomes an act of stewardship rather than a matter of urgency.

Authority must be clarified before it is delegated. When churches govern roles and approval thresholds faithfully, they protect alignment, accountability, and trust long before the first interview.

Chapter 5

Defining the Role Under Authority

A role that is not defined under authority cannot be governed in practice. Churches often create roles to meet immediate needs, relieve pressure, or respond to growth, but they fail to define those roles with sufficient clarity. When authority is assumed rather than specified, the role expands informally, expectations shift unpredictably, and accountability becomes difficult to enforce.

Defining a role under authority means more than listing tasks. It requires identifying what authority is being granted, where that authority begins and ends, and to whom the role is accountable. Without these elements, even well-intentioned staff members will operate according to personal judgment rather than shared standards. Over time, this produces inconsistency and conflict.

Roles must be defined in relation to governance, not personality. Churches often shape roles around the strengths or preferences of a particular individual. While this may seem practical, it undermines authority. When roles are person-dependent rather than value-governed, expectations become fluid, and correction feels personal. Authority should reside in the role itself, not in the individual who occupies it.

A clearly governed role establishes limits. It identifies decision rights and clarifies what decisions require approval. It specifies how success is measured beyond outcomes and identifies behaviors that are not permitted, even if they appear effective. These boundaries protect both the church and the individual serving within the role.

Defining the role under authority also establishes accountability pathways. Staff members must know who evaluates their work, how feedback is given, and how corrections are handled. When accountability is unclear, issues are delayed, tensions escalate, and trust erodes. Clear authority allows correction to occur early, fairly, and consistently.

Roles that involve teaching, counseling, discipline, financial stewardship, or public representation require heightened clarity. These functions carry greater influence and spiritual responsibility. Defining such roles without governance places undue risk on the church and unfair pressure on the individual serving.

Faithful churches define roles before they are filled. They establish authority before delegation. They clarify expectations before interviews begin. When roles are defined under authority, hiring decisions become disciplined acts of stewardship rather than reactive responses to need.

This chapter reinforces a foundational discipline. Authority must shape the role before the role shapes the church. Only then can hiring protect alignment, accountability, and trust over time.

Authority, Responsibility, And Accountability

Authority, responsibility, and accountability must exist together. When one is separated from the others, leadership becomes unstable, and correction becomes difficult. In the church, this imbalance often occurs unintentionally. Roles are created with responsibilities but without defined authority, or authority is granted without clear accountability. Both conditions produce confusion and risk.

Authority refers to the right to decide, direct, or act on behalf of the church. Responsibility refers to the work that must be carried out. Accountability refers to the process by which authority and responsibility are evaluated and corrected. A role is only governed when all three are clearly defined and aligned.

Problems arise when responsibility exceeds authority. Staff members are expected to lead, manage, or resolve issues without the authority to make necessary decisions. This creates frustration and delay. Individuals compensate by operating informally, bypassing leadership, or making unilateral decisions to meet expectations. Over time, informal authority replaces governed authority.

Equally dangerous is authority without responsibility. When individuals are granted decision-making power without clearly defined expectations, authority becomes unchecked. Outcomes are difficult to evaluate because responsibilities were never specified. Correction feels arbitrary because there is no agreed-upon standard. This imbalance invites misuse, whether intentional or not.

Accountability is the stabilizing force that binds authority and responsibility together. It clarifies who evaluates performance, how concerns are addressed, and when correction is required. Accountability must be active, not assumed. Regular feedback, defined evaluation criteria, and clear reporting relationships prevent small issues from becoming entrenched patterns.

In governed roles, authority is limited to what is necessary, responsibility is clearly articulated, and accountability is visible. Staff members know what decisions they can make, what outcomes they are responsible for, and who has the right to correct or redirect them. This clarity protects dignity while enabling discipline.

Defining authority, responsibility, and accountability before hiring begins is an act of stewardship. It prevents role drift, reduces conflict, and creates conditions for faithful service. When these elements are aligned, leadership becomes stable, correction becomes principled, and trust is preserved within the life of the church.

Ministry Function Vs. Leadership Authority

Ministry function and leadership authority are related but not the same. Churches often assume that performing ministry automatically confers leadership authority, or that leadership authority is required for all ministry functions. This confusion leads to misplaced influence, unclear accountability, and unnecessary risk.

Ministry function refers to the work the ministry performs. It includes serving, assisting, facilitating, and supporting the church's mission. Many ministry functions are vital and visible, but they do not require independent authority to shape direction, doctrine, or discipline. Faithful service does not always involve leadership authority.

Leadership authority, by contrast, involves discretion, decision-making, and representation on behalf of the church. It grants the right to interpret values, resolve conflict, direct others, and act with delegated power. Authority is present wherever judgment is exercised beyond prescribed tasks.

Problems arise when ministry functions are given leadership authority without necessity. Volunteers or staff may be empowered beyond their scope to meet immediate needs or avoid bottlenecks. While this may appear efficient, it often leads to inconsistent application of values and unclear lines of accountability.

Equally problematic is assigning leadership authority without acknowledging it. When individuals are expected to make decisions, handle sensitive issues, or influence others without formal recognition of authority, they operate in a gray area. Correction becomes difficult because the authority was never named or governed.

Faithful role design distinguishes clearly between function and authority. It identifies which tasks require discretion and which operate within established boundaries. It ensures that authority is granted intentionally, not accidentally, and that it is matched with appropriate accountability.

Understanding the difference between ministry function and leadership authority protects both the church and those who serve within it. It prevents unnecessary elevation, reduces confusion, and ensures that influence is stewarded carefully. When roles are designed with this distinction in mind, ministry can flourish without compromising governance or trust.

Staff Roles That Teach, Influence, Or Discipline

Certain staff roles carry inherent authority because they shape belief, behavior, and correction within the life of the church. These roles move beyond task execution and into spiritual and organizational influence. When a role teaches, influences, or disciplines, it must be governed with heightened care, regardless of whether it is labeled pastoral, administrative, or support.

Teaching authority is not limited to the pulpit. Staff members teach whenever they explain Scripture, lead groups, counsel individuals, answer theological questions, or model interpretation through practice. Teaching also occurs informally through tone, emphasis, and silence. When those entrusted with teaching roles are not clearly aligned with values and doctrine, confusion is introduced quietly and reinforced over time.

Influence extends beyond formal leadership titles. Staff members influence culture through daily decisions, interpersonal interactions, and responses to conflict. Those who set schedules, manage communication, coordinate volunteers, or resolve problems shape how the church functions and what behaviors are normalized. Influence exists wherever discretion is exercised and observed by others.

Disciplinary authority carries the greatest responsibility and risk. Discipline includes correction, redirection, and boundary enforcement. Staff members who address misconduct, mediate conflict, or enforce standards are exercising authority that directly affects trust and spiritual health. When disciplinary authority is unclear or inconsistently applied, correction feels personal rather than principled, and resentment follows.

These roles require explicit governance. Authority must be clearly defined, limited to what is necessary, and paired with visible accountability. Expectations must be documented, and oversight must be active. Without this structure, staff members are placed in positions of influence without protection, and the church is exposed to inconsistency and harm.

Faithful churches recognize that teaching, influence, and discipline are not incidental functions. They are governing activities. Roles that carry these responsibilities must be defined under authority, approved at appropriate levels, and staffed with individuals whose values, character, and maturity are evident.

When such roles are governed well, authority is exercised with clarity and restraint. Correction becomes restorative rather than reactive. Teaching strengthens rather than confuses. Influence builds trust rather than dependency. Governance at this level protects doctrine, culture, and witness by ensuring that authority is deliberately entrusted and faithfully stewarded.

Chapter 6
Writing Roles That Can Be Enforced

A role that cannot be enforced cannot be governed. Churches often write job descriptions that describe activities but avoid authority, boundaries, and consequences. These documents may communicate intent, but they do not establish standards. When enforcement is absent, accountability becomes subjective, and correction feels personal rather than principled.

Writing roles that can be enforced requires discipline. The purpose of a role description is not to attract candidates or appear flexible. It is to define authority, responsibility, and accountability clearly enough that expectations are unmistakable and correction is possible. Enforceable roles protect both the church and the individual serving within them.

Enforceable roles specify authority. They identify which decisions the role is permitted to make independently, which require approval, and where discretion ends. Without this clarity, authority expands informally, often in response to urgency or pressure. Once informal authority is established, it is difficult to correct without conflict.

Responsibilities must be defined in terms of outcomes and behaviors, not just tasks. Tasks describe activity. Outcomes and behaviors establish standards. A role that lists tasks without defining acceptable conduct or priorities cannot be evaluated meaningfully. When performance is assessed only by results, values are compromised.

Enforcement also requires defining what is not permitted. Many churches avoid negative language, fearing it appears ungracious. In reality, boundaries provide protection. Clearly stating prohibited behaviors, conflicts of interest, or instances of authority overreach prevents misunderstandings and reduces the need for reactive discipline.

Accountability mechanisms must be included. Enforceable roles identify who supervises the role, how feedback is given, and the process to follow when expectations are not met. Without this structure, leaders hesitate to correct, and issues persist until they become crises.

Writing roles that can be enforced does not create rigidity. It creates fairness. It ensures that correction is based on shared standards rather than personal preference. It allows leadership to act decisively while preserving dignity and trust.

Faithful churches invest time in writing enforceable roles before hiring begins. They understand that clarity at the outset prevents conflict later. When roles are written under authority and governed by values, enforcement becomes a tool for protection rather than punishment, and hiring becomes an act of stewardship rather than risk.

Why Vague Job Descriptions Undermine Accountability

Vague job descriptions create the illusion of flexibility while quietly eliminating accountability. When expectations are undefined or loosely stated, authority expands informally, and responsibility becomes difficult to measure. In the church, this ambiguity is often justified in the name of grace, teamwork, or adaptability, but the result is instability rather than unity.

Accountability depends on clarity. Leaders cannot evaluate performance, correct behavior, or enforce standards when expectations were never clearly articulated. When roles are vague, correction feels subjective. Staff members may resist feedback, not out of defiance, but because they were never given a clear standard against which to measure their conduct or decisions.

Vague descriptions also shift authority from governance to personality. In the absence of defined boundaries, individuals operate according to personal judgment, gifting, or relational influence. Those who are more assertive or effective naturally assume greater authority, while others withdraw. This creates uneven enforcement and resentment within teams.

Another consequence of vagueness is delayed correction. Leaders hesitate to address issues early because they are unsure whether expectations have truly been violated. Problems are tolerated until they escalate. When correction finally occurs, it feels abrupt and unfair, even when the behavior has been harmful for some time.

Vague job descriptions also undermine trust. Staff members may feel set up for failure when expectations change or are clarified only after problems arise. Congregants and volunteers sense inconsistency when leadership responses vary. Over time, confidence in leadership decision-making erodes.

Clear job descriptions do not eliminate the need for discernment, but they establish a shared foundation. They define authority, responsibility, and accountability in advance. When expectations are clear, correction becomes principled, discipline becomes restorative, and trust is preserved.

Faithful churches recognize that clarity is not unloving. It is protective. Writing roles with precision honors both the authority of leadership and the dignity of those who serve. Without clarity, accountability collapses, and the cost is paid through confusion, frustration, and weakened governance.

Non-Negotiables Tied To Values

Non-negotiables are the practical expression of values in action. They define what a church will not compromise, regardless of pressure, personality, effectiveness, or circumstance. When values are governed, non-negotiables provide the enforcement mechanism that protects doctrine, culture, and trust.

Many churches hesitate to articulate non-negotiables because they fear appearing rigid or ungracious. In reality, the absence of non-negotiables does not create flexibility; it creates inconsistency. Without clear limits, standards shift in response to urgency, relationships, or outcomes. Over time, values lose authority because nothing is actually enforced.

Non-negotiables tied to values clarify expectations before authority is granted. They establish boundaries around behavior, belief, and conduct that are not subject to reinterpretation. These boundaries do not exist to punish, but to protect. They protect the church from drift and protect the individual from operating in ambiguity.

In enforceable roles, non-negotiables should be explicit. They may include doctrinal alignment, moral conduct, relational integrity, submission to authority, confidentiality, or appropriate use of influence. These expectations must be observable and enforceable, not aspirational or implied. A non-negotiable that cannot be enforced is not a standard; it is a preference.

Tying non-negotiables directly to values removes personal bias from correction. When expectations are violated, leaders do not react emotionally or selectively. They are enforcing a standard that was clearly communicated and accepted. This allows discipline to be exercised consistently and redemptively rather than defensively.

Non-negotiables also create fairness. Everyone serving under authority is held to the same standards, regardless of role, tenure, or perceived effectiveness. This consistency strengthens trust within leadership teams and the congregation. It communicates that values apply to all, not only to the expendable.

Faithful churches do not wait for failure to clarify non-negotiables. They define them before hiring begins and incorporate them into role descriptions, evaluations, and corrective processes. When non-negotiables are clearly tied to values, authority is exercised with integrity, and governance is sustained over time.

"This Role Does Not Include" Language

Clear roles require clear limits. One of the most effective and underused tools for governance is explicitly stating what a role does not include. While churches are often comfortable describing responsibilities and expectations, they frequently avoid naming exclusions. This avoidance creates ambiguity, invites role drift, and undermines accountability.

"This role does not include" language functions as a boundary-setting mechanism. It clarifies where authority ends and prevents informal expansion driven by personality, urgency, or assumption. Without explicit exclusions, roles grow quietly. Staff members take on influence they were never assigned, and leaders hesitate to intervene because limits were never clearly stated.

Exclusion language is not restrictive. It is protective. It protects the church from unintended delegation of authority and protects the individual from pressure to operate outside their mandate. When staff members know what is not expected of them, they are less likely to overreach or feel responsible for outcomes beyond their authority.

This language is especially important in roles that intersect with teaching, counseling, discipline, or decision-making. For example, a role may support ministry leaders without setting doctrine, assist pastoral care without providing spiritual counseling, or manage logistics without directing volunteers independently. Without stating these limits, the role becomes vulnerable to misinterpretation.

Including "this role does not include" statements also strengthens enforcement. When issues arise, leaders can point to clearly documented boundaries rather than relying on subjective judgment. Correction becomes principled instead of personal. Accountability is grounded in agreed-upon definitions rather than evolving expectations.

Churches sometimes fear that exclusionary language communicates distrust. In practice, it communicates clarity and respect. It signals that authority is intentional and that governance is taken seriously. Staff members are more likely to serve confidently when they understand both their scope and their limits.

Faithful role design names responsibilities and exclusions with equal clarity. When “this role does not include” language is incorporated into job descriptions, authority is constrained appropriately, role drift is prevented, and accountability is preserved. Clear limits do not hinder ministry. They sustain it.

Discernment Questions for Establishing Hiring Authority

The questions below are designed to help churches evaluate whether hiring authority, role clarity, and governance are truly in place before a search begins. These questions are not meant to be asked only of candidates. Many of them should first be asked by elders, boards, pastors, and leadership teams themselves.

Used properly, these questions surface ambiguity early, before authority is delegated and expectations harden.

Questions For Church Leadership Before The Search

- Who has the formal right to approve this hire, and on what basis was that authority granted?
- What specific authority will this role exercise that could affect doctrine, culture, finances, discipline, or public witness?
- At what level does this hire become a governance decision rather than an operational one?
- What approval thresholds apply to this role, and who must be involved before an offer is extended?
- If this hire fails, who remains accountable for the decision?
- What values must govern this role that cannot be compromised under pressure or urgency?

Questions That Clarify Role, Authority, and Limits

- What decisions may this role make independently, and what decisions require approval?
- Where does this role's authority explicitly end?
- What responsibilities does this role carry that require accountability beyond task completion?
- How will success be evaluated beyond outcomes or performance metrics?

• What behaviors or actions would violate the authority entrusted to this role?
• What does this role not include, even if the individual is capable or willing?

Questions For Early Candidate Discernment

These questions may be asked of candidates only after leadership clarity has been established.
• How do you understand the difference between serving faithfully and exercising authority?
• Tell us about a time when your authority was limited by leadership. How did you respond?
• How do you handle responsibility when you are not given full decision-making authority?
• What boundaries do you believe should never be crossed in a church role, even when results are good?
• How do you respond when expectations are clearly defined but feel restrictive?
• What accountability do you believe is necessary for roles that influence others spiritually or organizationally?

How These Questions Should Be Used

These questions are not designed to produce polished answers. They are intended to reveal posture, understanding of authority, and alignment with governed values. Patterns matter more than individual responses. Discomfort, defensiveness, or vagueness often reveal more than confidence.

If leadership cannot answer the governance questions clearly, the church is not yet ready to hire. If candidates resist clarity of authority, they are not ready to receive authority.

Part III

Values Alignment and Spiritual Qualification

Once the hiring authority has been established and roles have been clearly defined under governance, the focus must shift to alignment. This stage is where many churches assume agreement rather than test it. Values alignment and spiritual qualification are not implied by shared faith language, denominational familiarity, or enthusiasm for ministry. They must be carefully discerned and deliberately confirmed.

Values alignment answers a different question than competence. It asks whether an individual will operate in accordance with the church's governing convictions when pressure, conflict, or sacrifice is required. Spiritual qualification addresses whether the individual's character, maturity, and private life are consistent with the authority they will be entrusted to carry. Together, these elements determine whether authority can be extended safely.

Churches often attempt to assess alignment solely through belief statements. While doctrinal agreement is necessary, it is not sufficient. Values are revealed through patterns of behavior, responses to correction, posture toward authority, and consistency between public ministry and private life. Alignment is demonstrated, not declared.

Spiritual qualification must be approached with both seriousness and care. Scripture provides clear standards for those who lead, teach, and influence the body. These standards exist to protect the church and the individual, not to create elitism or exclusion. Ignoring them does not produce grace. It produces vulnerability.

This section addresses how churches can evaluate values alignment without turning interviews into theological debates and how spiritual qualifications can be assessed without crossing ethical or legal boundaries. It provides guidance for distinguishing between essential doctrine and secondary differences, between character and charisma, and between maturity and giftedness.

Part III moves the hiring process from structure to discernment. Authority has been clarified. Roles have been defined. The question now becomes whether the individual under consideration is prepared to live within the values, boundaries, and accountability that faithful leadership requires.

The chapters that follow will examine values alignment, doctrinal fit, character, family life, and spiritual health with clarity and restraint. Faithful churches do not assume alignment. They confirm it before authority is ever entrusted.

Chapter 7
Values Alignment Is Not Optional

Values alignment is not a preference, a courtesy, or an added layer of discernment. It is a requirement for the faithful delegation of authority. When churches treat values alignment as optional, they invite instability, inconsistency, and conflict into leadership before the role is ever filled.

Shared faith language does not guarantee shared values. Agreement on doctrine does not ensure agreement on boundaries, authority, or behavior under pressure. Many hiring failures occur not because individuals reject a church's beliefs, but because they operate from a different set of governing convictions. These differences remain hidden until authority is exercised and expectations collide.

Values alignment determines how authority will be used when outcomes are uncertain, relationships are strained, or obedience is costly. It governs responses to correction, conflict, and compromise. Without alignment at this level, leadership becomes personality-driven rather than principle-driven, and enforcement feels personal rather than principled.

Churches often prioritize harmony during the hiring process, avoiding difficult questions out of a desire to be gracious or trusting. This avoidance is costly. Alignment that is not tested before authority is granted will be tested later through conflict. When this happens, correction feels abrupt, and trust is damaged, even when leaders act rightly.

Scripture consistently places alignment and character before appointment. Leaders were examined publicly, patiently, and carefully, not to exclude unnecessarily, but to protect the body. These standards reflect the seriousness of delegated authority. Ignoring them does not accelerate ministry. It weakens it.

Values alignment is not about finding perfect agreement on every issue. It is about confirming shared non-negotiables and a willingness to live within governed boundaries. When values alignment is clear, authority can be extended with confidence. When it is assumed, authority becomes a liability.

This chapter establishes a firm principle for the remainder of this section. Alignment is not optional because authority is not neutral. Faithful churches confirm values alignment before they entrust influence, responsibility, and representation to anyone within the life of the church.

Core Convictions Versus Preferences

A critical failure point in church hiring occurs when core convictions are treated as preferences or when preferences are elevated to the level of conviction. Both errors distort discernment and undermine governance. Faithful values alignment requires a disciplined distinction between what is essential and what is negotiable.

Core convictions are non-negotiable beliefs and values that govern doctrine, authority, behavior, and accountability. They shape how Scripture is interpreted, how leadership is exercised, and how correction is handled. These convictions must be shared by anyone entrusted with authority because they define the boundaries within which the church operates. When core convictions are compromised, alignment collapses regardless of competence or sincerity.

Preferences, by contrast, involve style, methodology, personality, and secondary theological emphases. They influence how ministry is expressed but not what it protects. Preferences vary across leaders, cultures, and seasons, and they must be held with humility. Treating preferences as convictions creates unnecessary exclusion, fosters uniformity over unity, and often masks insecurity rather than faithfulness.

Churches frequently blur this distinction during hiring. Candidates may be rejected over stylistic differences while deeper convictions go unexamined. Conversely, individuals may be welcomed because they align with cultural preferences while differing on authority, accountability, or doctrinal boundaries. Both approaches misplace emphasis and expose the church to risk.

Values alignment focuses on convictions, not comfort. It asks whether an individual shares the church's governing beliefs about Scripture, authority, discipline, moral conduct, and stewardship. It examines how those convictions are lived, not merely affirmed. Preferences may affect chemistry, but convictions determine trustworthiness.

Scripture models this distinction clearly. Unity in the church is grounded in shared truth and obedience, not uniform expression. Leaders are called to guard doctrine and live blamelessly, not to replicate personality or style. When churches confuse preference with conviction, they either fracture unnecessarily or compromise dangerously.

Faithful hiring requires restraint and clarity. Core convictions must be identified, articulated, and enforced. Preferences must be acknowledged and held loosely. When this distinction is honored, churches can extend authority confidently without demanding conformity or risking compromise.

Cultural Alignment Without Cloning

Cultural alignment is often misunderstood as sameness. Churches sometimes assume that alignment requires similar personalities, backgrounds, communication styles, or ministry approaches. This assumption leads to cloning rather than discernment and ultimately weakens the body rather than strengthening it.

Cultural alignment refers to shared commitments about how authority is exercised, how people are treated, how conflict is handled, and how values are lived out in daily ministry. It is not about personal chemistry or stylistic compatibility. It is about whether an individual will reinforce the church's governing values through consistent behavior.

Cloning occurs when churches prioritize familiarity over faithfulness. Leaders gravitate toward candidates who look like them, think like them, or lead like them. While this may feel safe, it narrows perspective and reduces accountability. Uniform personalities often reinforce blind spots rather than challenge them.

True cultural alignment allows for difference. It welcomes diversity of gifting, experience, and expression while remaining anchored to shared convictions. Aligned individuals may disagree, innovate, or approach ministry differently, but they do so within clearly governed boundaries. Their differences strengthen the church because values, not personalities, provide cohesion.

Misalignment becomes visible not through difference, but through resistance to authority, discomfort with accountability, or disregard for established boundaries. These indicators matter more than stylistic fit. A candidate who respects governance and aligns with values will contribute positively, even when their approach differs from existing leadership.

Scripture presents the church as a body with many members, not replicas of one another. Unity is grounded in shared truth and obedience, not sameness. Cultural alignment without cloning honors this design by preserving both faithfulness and diversity.

Faithful churches resist the temptation to hire for comfort. They hire for alignment. When values govern culture, diversity becomes an asset rather than a threat, and authority is strengthened rather than diluted.

Why Disagreement Must Be Surfaced Before Hiring

Disagreement is not the problem. Unexamined disagreement is. Churches often avoid surfacing differences during the hiring process out of a desire to be gracious, unified, or hopeful. This avoidance does not create harmony. It postpones conflict until authority has already been granted, when correction becomes more costly, and trust is harder to preserve.

Hiring introduces authority into the life of the church. Once authority is delegated, disagreement is no longer theoretical. It affects decisions, direction, and behavior. When differences in conviction, interpretation, or values remain undisclosed during the hiring process, they surface later through resistance, tension, or quiet noncompliance. By that point, leaders are correcting someone they have already affirmed, which feels relationally fraught and spiritually confusing.

Surfacing disagreement before hiring is an act of honesty and protection. It allows both the church and the candidate to evaluate alignment without pressure. Candidates can speak openly about convictions, concerns, and boundaries without fear of jeopardizing a role they already occupy. Churches can discern whether differences fall within acceptable variance or represent fundamental misalignment.

Disagreements that are surfaced early can be addressed calmly and clearly. Expectations can be clarified. Boundaries can be defined. In some cases, differences can be resolved through understanding and agreement. In others, they reveal that authority should not be delegated. Neither outcome is a failure. Both are faithful.

Avoiding disagreement often stems from fear. Leaders fear losing a strong candidate. Candidates fear appearing difficult. This mutual caution creates superficial agreement that cannot withstand the weight of real ministry. When pressure arrives, what was avoided becomes unavoidable.

Scripture does not call leaders to eliminate disagreement, but to handle it truthfully and wisely. Unity is preserved through shared conviction and clear boundaries, not through silence. When disagreement is surfaced before hiring, alignment is tested rather than assumed, and authority is entrusted with clarity rather than hope.

Faithful churches do not fear disagreement during discernment. They recognize it as a gift that reveals whether shared values are real. By addressing differences before authority is granted, churches protect doctrine, culture, and trust long before correction would be required.

Chapter 8
Doctrine, Belief, and Teaching Authority

Doctrine is not merely a statement of belief. It is the framework through which Scripture is interpreted, authority is exercised, and truth is applied to life. When a church entrusts its teaching authority without clear doctrinal alignment, it risks confusion, inconsistency, and drift, even when intentions are sincere.

Teaching authority exists wherever Scripture is explained, applied, or modeled. This authority is exercised from pulpits, classrooms, counseling rooms, small groups, and informal conversations. It also operates through decisions about what to emphasize, what to avoid, and how to handle difficult passages. Teaching authority shapes belief not only by what is said, but by what is consistently reinforced.

Belief statements alone are insufficient to govern teaching authority. Many candidates can affirm doctrinal language without sharing the same interpretive framework or convictions about application. Differences may not appear immediately, especially when teaching is general or introductory. Over time, however, subtle shifts in emphasis, tone, or omission reshape the church's theological center.

Churches must therefore distinguish between assent and alignment. Assent acknowledges agreement in principle. Alignment reflects shared conviction about how doctrine governs life, leadership, discipline, and authority. Teaching authority requires alignment, not merely affirmation.

Doctrinal alignment must also account for the scope of influence. Not every role requires the same level of doctrinal precision.

Roles that teach Scripture, disciple others, or counsel spiritually require deeper alignment than roles that support ministry operationally. The greater the teaching authority, the greater the requirement for clarity, maturity, and accountability.

Problems arise when teaching authority is assumed rather than defined. Staff members may teach implicitly through advice, prayer, or example, without realizing they are exercising authority. Without governance, leaders hesitate to correct doctrinal inconsistencies because authority boundaries have never been established. Correction then feels personal rather than principled.

Scripture consistently emphasizes the seriousness of teaching. Those who teach are held to a higher standard because their influence shapes belief and practice. This standard exists to protect the church, not to unnecessarily restrict ministry. When churches minimize doctrinal alignment in the name of unity or effectiveness, they weaken the very foundation that sustains both.

Faithful churches govern teaching authority carefully. They clarify which roles teach, what doctrine must be upheld, and how alignment will be evaluated and maintained. When doctrine, belief, and teaching authority are aligned under governance, truth is preserved, trust is strengthened, and leadership serves with clarity rather than confusion.

Teaching authority must be entrusted deliberately, governed by shared conviction, and protected through accountability. Without this care, belief becomes fragmented, and the church pays a cost that is difficult to repair.

Distinguishing Essential Doctrine From Secondary Matters

Faithful governance requires discernment, not uniformity. One of the most difficult and necessary disciplines in church hiring is distinguishing between essential doctrine that must be shared and secondary matters where diversity of thought may exist without undermining unity or authority. Confusing these categories either fractures the church unnecessarily or exposes it to doctrinal compromise.

Essential doctrine consists of truths that define the faith and govern the church's identity, authority, and witness. These doctrines shape how Scripture is understood, how salvation is proclaimed, how authority is exercised, and how holiness and discipline are applied. Disagreement on essential doctrine is not a matter of preference. It represents misalignment that makes shared authority impossible.

Secondary matters involve theological interpretation, methodology, or emphasis that do not alter the core of the gospel or the church's governing convictions. These differences may affect teaching style, ministry approach, or personal conscience, but they do not redefine the church's theological foundation. Faithful churches allow room for such differences while maintaining clear boundaries around essentials.

Problems arise when churches fail to name which doctrines are essential. In the absence of clarity, leaders either avoid theological questions altogether or elevate personal convictions to the level of orthodoxy. Both approaches undermine governance. Avoidance allows drift. Overreach creates division.

In hiring, this distinction must be explicit. Candidates should know which doctrines are non-negotiable and which areas allow charitable disagreement. This clarity protects both parties. It prevents candidates from assuming alignment where none exists and prevents churches from discovering fundamental differences after authority has already been granted.

The teaching authority increases the importance of this distinction. Those who teach Scripture must be aligned on essential doctrine and willing to submit to the church's interpretive boundaries. Disagreement on secondary matters may be discussed and even explored, but it must never be used to undermine unity or authority.

Scripture itself models this distinction. Core truths are guarded firmly, while secondary matters are addressed with patience and restraint. This balance preserves both truth and peace. When churches collapse these categories, they either compromise doctrine or fracture community.

Faithful churches do not demand agreement on everything. They demand alignment on what governs everything. Distinguishing essential doctrine from secondary matters allows authority to be entrusted without confusion and diversity to exist without disorder.

Teaching Roles Versus Service Roles

Not every role in the church carries the same doctrinal weight. Faithful hiring requires a clear distinction between teaching roles and service roles, not to diminish the importance of service, but to recognize the differing levels of authority and responsibility each carries. Confusing these roles exposes the church to unnecessary risk and places individuals into expectations they were never meant to bear.

Teaching roles exercise direct influence over belief, interpretation, and spiritual formation. These roles include preaching, teaching classes, leading small groups, discipling others, counseling spiritually, and any position where Scripture is explained or applied with authority. Teaching roles shape how the congregation understands truth, obedience, and discipleship. Because of this influence, teaching roles require a higher level of doctrinal alignment, spiritual maturity, and accountability.

By contrast, service roles, support the church's mission through assistance, coordination, hospitality, administration, and care. These roles are vital to the life of the church, but they do not require independent doctrinal authority. Service roles operate within established boundaries and direction rather than defining or interpreting them. Faithful service does not depend on the authority of teaching.

Problems arise when churches blur this distinction. Service roles may unintentionally become teaching roles through informal counseling, unchecked influence, or assumed authority. Conversely, individuals in teaching roles may be treated as service staff, expected to execute tasks without recognition of the authority and responsibility they carry. Both situations create confusion and undermine governance.

A clear role definition protects everyone involved. Those serving in teaching roles understand the weight of authority they are entrusted with and the standards they are expected to uphold. Those serving in service roles are protected from being pressured into responsibilities beyond their scope. Accountability becomes appropriate rather than excessive or absent.

This distinction also prevents doctrinal drift. When teaching authority is limited to roles designed to carry it, belief remains anchored, and correction is clear. When everyone is allowed to teach informally without governance, doctrine becomes fragmented, and enforcement becomes impossible.

Scripture affirms both teaching and service as essential functions within the body, but it assigns them different responsibilities and standards. Faithful churches honor this distinction by governing teaching roles carefully and valuing service roles without burdening them with authority they were never meant to carry.

When teaching clearly distinguishes roles and service roles, the church operates with clarity, unity, and integrity. Authority is exercised intentionally, service is honored properly, and doctrine is protected without suppressing faithful participation.

How Doctrinal Misalignment Begins

Doctrinal misalignment rarely begins with open disagreement or intentional deception. It most often begins quietly, through assumptions, omissions, and unexamined differences that coexist under the banner of unity. By the time conflict becomes visible, authority has already been delegated, and correction has become difficult.

Misalignment often starts with vague agreement. Candidates affirm belief statements using shared language, but underlying interpretive frameworks differ. Words such as grace, authority, obedience, repentance, or freedom are used similarly but understood differently. Because alignment is assumed rather than tested, these differences remain hidden during the hiring process.

Another common entry point is informal teaching. Individuals in non-teaching roles begin offering counsel, advice, or spiritual guidance beyond their scope of practice. These interactions may be well-intentioned, but they introduce theological assumptions that have not been governed or reviewed. Over time, informal teaching carries as much influence as formal instruction, especially when it is relational and trusted.

Doctrinal misalignment also begins when enforcement is avoided. Leaders may recognize minor inconsistencies but choose not to address them out of a desire to preserve harmony or avoid conflict. This silence communicates permission. What is tolerated quietly becomes normalized publicly. The issue is no longer what the church believes, but what it allows to be taught or practiced.

Pressure accelerates misalignment. When growth, attendance, or effectiveness are prioritized over clarity, leaders compromise enforcement to maintain momentum. Individuals who produce visible results are given latitude that others do not. Doctrine is reshaped by outcomes rather than convictions, even when belief statements remain unchanged.

Another contributor is unclear teaching authority. When roles that influence belief are not clearly defined, no one is certain who has the right to correct or clarify doctrine. Responsibility diffuses. Correction is delayed. By the time authority is asserted, resistance has already formed.

Doctrinal misalignment is rarely dramatic at first. It develops through small decisions made without governance. Each unaddressed deviation shifts the center slightly until the church no longer recognizes how far it has moved.

Faithful churches recognize that doctrine must be governed, not assumed. Alignment must be examined, not implied. By addressing misalignment early, before authority is entrenched, churches protect truth, unity, and trust without resorting to crisis correction later.

Chapter 9
Character, Family, and Private Life

Character is not an accessory to leadership. It is the foundation that determines whether authority can be carried without harm. In the church, hiring decisions that ignore character, family life, and private conduct place the congregation, the individual, and the gospel witness at risk. These areas are not secondary considerations. They are biblical requirements.

Scripture consistently links leadership authority to observable character. Qualifications for those who lead emphasize self-control, humility, faithfulness, and integrity, not public success or giftedness. These qualities are not situational. They are revealed over time through patterns of behavior, especially when no one is watching. A candidate's private life will eventually shape their public ministry.

Family life is a visible extension of character, not a separate category. Scripture treats the household as a proving ground for leadership because it reveals how authority, care, correction, and responsibility are exercised in daily life. This does not require perfection, but it does require consistency, faithfulness, and accountability. Ignoring family life in hiring decisions removes a key indicator Scripture itself provides.

Churches often hesitate to address these areas for fear of appearing intrusive or judgmental. This hesitation is understandable, but it is misplaced. Avoiding these considerations does not create grace. It creates blindness. When character and private life are left unexamined, issues surface later through moral failure, relational breakdown, or compromised authority, at a far greater cost.

Private conduct matters because leadership authority amplifies influence. Patterns of secrecy, unmanaged sin, unresolved conflict, or lack of accountability do not remain private once authority is entrusted. Pressure exposes what already exists. Without values governance, leaders may excuse warning signs in the name of effectiveness or potential.

This chapter does not argue for perfection or unrealistic standards. It argues for honesty and alignment. Churches must assess whether an individual's life reflects the values the church is committed to upholding and whether the individual is willing to live under accountability. Willingness to be examined is itself an indicator of maturity.

Faithful churches approach character, family, and private life with both seriousness and care. They ask clear questions, listen patiently, and discern patterns rather than isolated moments. They recognize that protecting the church begins with protecting those who lead it from being placed into authority they are not prepared to carry.

This chapter establishes a critical truth. Authority does not sanctify character. Character must precede authority. When churches govern hiring with this conviction, leadership becomes stable, correction becomes possible, and trust is preserved over time.

Biblical Qualifications

Biblical qualifications for leadership are not cultural suggestions or historical artifacts. They are governing standards given to protect the church, preserve doctrine, and safeguard those who lead. When churches treat these qualifications as optional or symbolic, they undermine the very authority Scripture establishes for leadership within the body.

Scripture emphasizes who a leader is before what a leader does. Qualifications focus on character, self-control, faithfulness, relational integrity, and spiritual maturity. These qualities are observable and enduring. They are designed to reveal whether an individual can carry authority without abusing it or being consumed by it.

Biblical qualifications are not benchmarks of perfection. They are indicators of a pattern. Scripture does not require flawlessness, but it does require consistency, repentance, and accountability. A leader's life should demonstrate ongoing submission to Christ and evidence of growth in holiness. Where sin exists, it must be addressed. Where weakness remains, it must be governed.

These qualifications also function as safeguards against haste. Scripture repeatedly warns against appointing leaders too quickly. Time allows patterns to emerge and character to be tested. When churches rush hiring decisions to meet urgency or fill gaps, they bypass the very protections Scripture provides.

Biblical qualifications apply proportionally to authority. The greater the influence, the higher the standard. Those entrusted with teaching, counseling, discipline, or public representation must meet clear and observable criteria. Lowering standards for the sake of effectiveness does not produce grace. It produces vulnerability.

Churches often struggle to apply biblical qualifications because they fear disqualifying sincere or gifted individuals. This fear misunderstands the purpose of qualification. Standards exist not to exclude unnecessarily, but to ensure that authority is entrusted safely and responsibly. Saying 'not yet' or 'not this role' is not rejection. It is stewardship.

Applying biblical qualifications faithfully requires clarity and courage. Churches must define what qualifies and disqualifies leadership roles, communicate these standards openly, and enforce them consistently. When qualifications are governed rather than ignored, leadership becomes stable, correction becomes possible, and trust is preserved.

Biblical qualifications remind the church of a foundational truth. Authority is sacred. It must be entrusted carefully, evaluated honestly, and governed by standards that do not shift with convenience or pressure.

Household Leadership And Witness

Scripture consistently treats the household as a proving ground for leadership, not as a private compartment separated from public ministry. How an individual leads, loves, disciplines, and serves within their home reveals how they will exercise authority within the church. Household leadership is not about image or control. It is about faithfulness, responsibility, and credibility.

Household leadership reflects the application of values in daily life. It shows how authority is exercised when relationships are close, emotions are involved, and outcomes are not visible to others. Patience, self-control, humility, and consistency cannot be staged in the home. They are either present or absent. For this reason, Scripture treats household faithfulness as a meaningful indicator of leadership readiness.

Witness is inseparable from household leadership. The church does not evaluate homes for perfection, but it must evaluate them for integrity. A household marked by chaos, neglect, unresolved conflict, or persistent inconsistency raises questions about how authority is being stewarded. These realities do not automatically disqualify someone, but they do require careful discernment, accountability, and, in some cases, restraint.

Churches often avoid examining household leadership out of fear of being intrusive or unfair. This avoidance misunderstands Scripture's intent. Household evaluation is not about policing private life. It is about recognizing patterns that affect public authority. Ignoring this dimension does not protect families or leaders. It exposes them to pressure they may not be prepared to carry.

Household leadership also affects witnesses beyond the church. Family members observe and experience how faith is lived under authority. When public ministry contradicts private conduct, credibility suffers. The gospel message is weakened when leadership authority is disconnected from lived example.

Faithful governance approaches household leadership with care and balance. It acknowledges complexity, offers support, and distinguishes between temporary struggles and entrenched patterns. It also recognizes that some seasons of life may limit readiness for certain forms of authority, even when gifting and desire are present.

Scripture's emphasis on household leadership is not restrictive. It is protective. It guards the church from entrusting authority prematurely and guards leaders from being placed into roles that strain their faith, family, and witness. When household leadership is examined honestly and graciously, authority can be extended with confidence rather than assumption.

Social Media And Public Representation

Public representation is no longer limited to physical presence or formal communication. Social media has become an extension of personal voice and public witness. For those serving under church authority, online conduct serves as public representation, whether intended or not. What is shared, endorsed, mocked, or normalized online communicates values and shapes perception.

Social media reveals posture. It exposes how individuals speak when not constrained by formal settings, how they handle disagreement, and what they choose to amplify; tone, frequency, and content matter. Patterns of sarcasm, hostility, moral ambiguity, or careless speech do not remain isolated online behaviors. They reflect how authority is likely to be exercised elsewhere.

Churches often hesitate to consider social media in hiring decisions, fearing intrusion or overreach. This hesitation is misplaced. Social media content is public by design. Evaluating public representation does not violate privacy. It is a necessary assessment of how an individual represents themselves and, by extension, the church when entrusted with influence.

Public representation includes more than controversy. It includes how leaders speak about Scripture, authority, sexuality, politics, culture, and conflict. It includes what they celebrate and what they remain silent about. Inconsistencies between stated values and public expression create confusion and weaken trust.

Social media also accelerates the consequences of misalignment. Statements made casually can spread quickly, be misunderstood, or be weaponized. When a staff member's online presence contradicts the church's values or doctrine, leadership is forced to resort to reactive correction. Without prior governance, responses feel defensive, and credibility suffers.

This does not require uniformity of opinion or silence on complex issues. It requires restraint, wisdom, and alignment with the church's values. Individuals entrusted with authority must understand that their public voice carries weight beyond personal expression. Willingness to submit online conduct to values governance is an indicator of maturity.

Faithful churches address social media and public representation before granting authority. Expectations are clarified. Boundaries are defined. Accountability is established. This protects both the church and the individual from preventable conflict.

Public representation is not optional for leaders. It is unavoidable. When values govern social media conduct, authority is exercised with integrity, witness is preserved, and trust is strengthened rather than strained.

Discernment Questions for Values Alignment and Spiritual Qualification

The questions at the conclusion of Part III are designed to surface alignment, not agreement. They are not meant to test theological sophistication or ministry experience. They are intended to reveal governing convictions, patterns of character, and readiness to live under authority.

These questions should be used carefully, prayerfully, and patiently. Patterns matter more than polished answers. Discomfort, defensiveness, or ambiguity often reveal more than confidence.

Questions for Church Leadership Before Evaluating Candidates

- What values are truly non-negotiable for this role, and have they been clearly articulated?
- Which spiritual qualifications are required for this role based on Scripture, not preference?
- What level of doctrinal alignment is necessary given the authority this role will carry?
- Are we willing to pause or stop the process if misalignment is revealed, even under pressure?
- Have we distinguished clearly between essential doctrine and secondary matters for this role?
- Are we prepared to enforce these standards consistently after the hire is made?

Questions That Surface Values Alignment

- When faithfulness and effectiveness are in tension, how do you decide which takes priority?
- Tell us about a time when you were asked to operate within boundaries you did not fully agree with. How did you respond?

• What values do you believe must never be compromised in church leadership, regardless of results?
• How do you respond when leadership corrects behavior rather than outcomes?
• What does submission to authority look like when you believe leadership may be wrong?
Questions That Discern Doctrinal and Teaching Alignment
• How do you determine what is essential doctrine versus secondary conviction?
• Describe how you handle Scripture when you encounter a passage that challenges your assumptions.
• In what situations do you believe disagreement should be voiced, and in what situations should it be restrained?
• How do you ensure that your teaching or counsel remains aligned with the church's doctrine rather than personal emphasis?
• What responsibility do you believe comes with teaching or influencing others spiritually?

Questions That Examine Character, Household, and Private Life

• How do you pursue accountability in your personal and spiritual life?
• What practices help you maintain integrity when no one is watching?
• How do you handle conflict or correction within close relationships?
• What pressures in your current season of life might affect your ability to carry this role faithfully?
• How do you discern when a season of life may limit readiness for certain responsibilities?

Questions Regarding Public Representation and Witness

• How do you decide what to share publicly, especially on social media?
• What boundaries guide your public voice when addressing controversial or sensitive issues?

- How do you respond if leadership asks you to adjust public behavior or communication?
- What responsibility do you believe leaders carry in representing the church beyond official settings?

How These Questions Should Be Used

These questions are not pass-fail tests. They are alignment tools. They are designed to reveal a posture toward authority, a willingness to live within governed values, and a readiness to carry influence responsibly.

If the alignment of values and spiritual qualifications is unclear, authority should not be delegated. Delay is not failure; it is protection.

Part III reinforces central discipline. Alignment must be confirmed before authority is entrusted. The next section will address how discernment moves into structured evaluation, verification, and protection as the hiring process continues.

Part IV
The Discernment and Interview Process

Discernment is not instinct, and interviewing is not intuition. Faithful church hiring requires both spiritual sensitivity and disciplined structure. When either is absent, decisions become reactive, inconsistent, or overly subjective. Part IV establishes how discernment is exercised responsibly through a governed interview process.

Many churches rely heavily on spiritual language during interviews, assuming that prayerful conversation alone will reveal alignment. Others rely on resumes, references, and impressions, assuming competence implies readiness. Both approaches fall short. Discernment without structure invites bias. Structure without discernment becomes mechanical. Faithful hiring requires both working together under authority.

The interview process is where values, authority, and alignment are tested in real time. This is not the stage for selling the role or rushing toward consensus. It is the stage for listening carefully, asking disciplined questions, and observing posture under pressure. Interviews reveal not only what candidates believe, but how they think, respond, and submit when authority and boundaries are made clear.

Governed interviews are intentional. They progress in stages. Early conversations surface posture and alignment. Later conversations test readiness, maturity, and accountability. At no point should urgency override discernment. A slowed process is not a lack of faith. It is an act of stewardship.

This section addresses how churches can design interview processes that are consistent, fair, and spiritually responsible. It explains how prayer and structure work together, why multi-stage interviews matter, and how questions should be framed to reveal alignment rather than rehearsed answers. It also addresses the roles of panels, teaching demonstrations, and reference checks within a disciplined discernment process.

Part IV moves the hiring process from alignment to confirmation. Authority has been clarified. Values have been examined. Spiritual qualification has been assessed. The question now is whether the individual demonstrates readiness to carry authority under real conditions.

The chapters that follow will provide practical guidance for designing interviews that protect the church, honor candidates, and support leaders in making faithful rather than impulsive decisions.

Chapter 10
Designing a Discernment Process

Discernment in church hiring is not a moment. It is a process. When churches treat discernment as a feeling or a single conversation, they reduce a governing responsibility to intuition. Faithful discernment requires structure, patience, and clarity so that spiritual sensitivity is exercised responsibly rather than impulsively.

A discernment process exists to slow decisions appropriately. Urgency is often the enemy of wisdom. Needs feel pressing. Roles feel empty. Ministry feels constrained. In these moments, churches are tempted to compress discernment into a brief exchange and spiritualize the outcome. This approach confuses faith with haste. Scripture consistently affirms patience, testing, and examination before authority is entrusted.

Designing a discernment process begins with intent. Leaders must decide in advance that alignment matters more than speed and that clarity matters more than convenience. This decision shapes the entire process. Interviews are no longer transactional. They become evaluative. Conversations are not about convincing candidates to join, but about discerning whether authority can be entrusted safely.

A disciplined discernment process is staged. Early stages focus on posture, values, and understanding of authority. The middle stages examine doctrine, character, and readiness. Later stages confirm alignment through observation, reference checks, and accountability discussion. Each stage serves a distinct purpose. Skipping stages increases risk and places undue weight on incomplete information.

Prayer is essential throughout the process, but prayer does not replace structure. Prayer guides wisdom. Structure disciplines it. When leaders pray and plan together, discernment is shared rather than kept to themselves. This protects against personal bias, emotional attachment, and overreliance on first impressions.

A governed discernment process also creates fairness. Candidates are evaluated consistently rather than subjectively. Expectations are communicated clearly. Decisions are documented and defensible. This transparency protects both the church and the individual, especially when alignment is not confirmed, and the process must end without an offer.

Designing a discernment process requires agreement among those with hiring authority. Elders, boards, pastors, and delegated leaders must align on stages, criteria, and decision thresholds before interviews begin. Without this agreement, discernment fragments and authority are exercised inconsistently.

Faithful churches do not rush discernment. They design it. They recognize that authority once granted is difficult to retract without harm. A disciplined discernment process protects doctrine, culture, and trust by ensuring that decisions are made deliberately, prayerfully, and under governance rather than pressure.

This chapter establishes a critical discipline for the remainder of the hiring process. Discernment must be intentional, structured, and shared. When designed well, it becomes a safeguard rather than a gamble, allowing churches to hire with confidence rather than hope.

Prayer, Wisdom, And Structure

Prayer, wisdom, and structure are not competing approaches to discernment. They are complementary disciplines that must work together for hiring decisions to be sound and faithful. When one is elevated at the expense of the others, discernment becomes distorted.

Prayer acknowledges dependence on God. It seeks clarity, humility, and restraint. In church hiring, prayer rightly frames the process as spiritual stewardship rather than organizational convenience. It reminds leaders that authority is not theirs to wield carelessly and that wisdom must be sought rather than assumed.

Wisdom applies truth to reality. It discerns patterns, weighs consequences, and resists impulse. Wisdom asks not only whether something is possible, but whether it is prudent. It recognizes that good intentions do not negate risk and that sincerity does not guarantee readiness. Wisdom bridges prayer and action by interpreting what faithfulness requires in practical terms.

Structure disciplines both prayer and wisdom. It prevents discernment from becoming subjective, rushed, or personality-driven. Structure establishes stages, criteria, and decision points that protect leaders from relying too heavily on impressions or emotions. It ensures that prayerful insight is tested over time rather than acted on prematurely.

Churches sometimes frame the structure of the church as a lack of faith. This is a false dichotomy. Scripture consistently pairs prayer with counsel, patience, and examination. Structure does not replace reliance on God. It honors it by refusing to confuse spiritual language with spiritual maturity.

When structure is absent, prayer can be used to justify haste. Leaders may claim peace where there has been little testing or agreement. Wisdom is then reduced to instinct, and accountability is weakened. When structure is present without prayer, the process becomes mechanical and detached from spiritual responsibility. When prayer, wisdom, and structure operate together, discernment is both reverent and reliable.

Faithful hiring requires all three. Prayer seeks God's guidance. Wisdom interprets circumstances faithfully. Structure ensures that neither is distorted by urgency, fear, or bias. Together, they form a discernment process that protects the church, honors candidates, and treats authority with the seriousness it deserves.

This balance reinforces the purpose of a governed discernment process. Hiring is not an act of faithlessness when done carefully. It is an act of obedience when prayer, wisdom, and structure are held together under authority.

Multi-Stage Interviews

Multi-stage interviews are not an administrative burden. They are a governance safeguard. When churches rely on a single conversation or informal meeting to make hiring decisions, they compress discernment into an unrealistic timeframe and place undue weight on first impressions. Faithful hiring requires time, repetition, and observation.

Each stage of the interview process serves a distinct purpose. Early conversations surface posture, values alignment, and understanding of authority. These conversations should be exploratory rather than evaluative, allowing both the church and the candidate to speak openly without pressure. At this stage, misalignment should halt the process without embarrassment or defensiveness.

The middle stages test readiness. Doctrine, character, and role understanding are examined in greater detail. Candidates are asked to engage specific scenarios, respond to boundaries, and articulate how they would operate under authority. These stages reveal patterns of thought and behavior that cannot be observed in an initial meeting.

Later stages confirm alignment rather than discover it. Teaching demonstrations, group interactions, reference checks, and accountability discussions belong here. By this point, the question is not whether the candidate is capable, but whether they can be consistently trusted with authority over time.

Multi-stage interviews protect against emotional momentum. As conversations progress, rapport naturally increases. Without structure, this rapport can create pressure to proceed even when concerns emerge. Staged processes allow leaders to pause, reflect, and confer before moving forward. They also create natural exit points when alignment is not confirmed.

This approach also protects candidates. Expectations are clarified gradually. Authority is discussed openly. Candidates are given time to consider whether the role and governance structure are a good fit for them. No one is rushed into a position they may later regret.

Scripture affirms the wisdom of testing over time. Leaders are not appointed hastily because character and alignment require observation. Multi-stage interviews operationalize this principle in a modern context.

Faithful churches design interview processes that unfold intentionally. They resist urgency, honor patience, and treat authority as something to be earned rather than assumed. When interviews are staged, discernment becomes disciplined, and hiring decisions are made with confidence rather than impulse.

Why "We Felt Peace" Is Insufficient Alone

Peace is a gift from God, but it is not a hiring methodology. When churches rely on statements such as "we felt peace" as the primary justification for a hiring decision, they confuse spiritual comfort with spiritual confirmation. Peace may accompany wise decisions, but it is not a substitute for discernment, testing, and governance.

Feelings of peace often arise from relief rather than alignment. A role has been filled. Pressure has eased. Conflict has been avoided. Momentum can continue. In these moments, peace reflects emotional resolution rather than spiritual validation. Without structure, peace becomes a way to sanctify urgency rather than restrain it.

Scripture does not present peace as an independent decision-making authority. Peace is repeatedly paired with wisdom, counsel, obedience, and patience. When peace is detached from testing, it becomes subjective and vulnerable to bias. Different leaders may feel peace at different times for different reasons, leaving no shared standard for accountability.

Relying on peace alone also silences necessary questions. Concerns may be dismissed as a lack of faith. Hesitation may be interpreted as resistance to the Spirit. This dynamic pressures leaders into agreement and discourages honest discernment. Over time, "we felt peace" becomes a conversation-ending phrase rather than a discernment checkpoint.

Peace that follows disciplined discernment is different. It is not immediate or euphoric. It is settled, informed, and shared. It emerges after values have been tested, authority clarified, alignment confirmed, and concerns addressed. This kind of peace does not eliminate responsibility. It accompanies it.

When hiring decisions are later questioned, peace alone offers no protection against governance. It cannot be evaluated, enforced, or revisited. Structure provides memory. Documentation provides clarity. Shared criteria provide accountability. Peace, without these supports, leaves leaders unable to explain or defend their decision faithfully.

Faithful churches honor peace without idolizing it. They treat peace as confirmation, not authorization. Discernment must be disciplined before it is declared complete. When peace follows wisdom, prayer, and structure, it strengthens confidence. When peace replaces them, it creates vulnerability.

Authority is too serious to be entrusted to feeling alone. Peace is meaningful, but it must be accompanied by tested alignment and governed discernment if hiring decisions are to protect doctrine, culture, and trust over time.

Chapter 11
Asking Questions That Reveal Alignment

The quality of a hiring decision is shaped largely by the quality of the questions asked. Churches often ask questions that gather information but fail to reveal alignment. Resumes, testimonies, and ministry stories provide context, but they do not expose how authority will be exercised, how values will be upheld, or how correction will be received. Faithful discernment requires questions that are designed to surface posture, conviction, and patterns of response.

Questions that reveal alignment are intentional. They move beyond what a candidate has done and focus on how they think, decide, and submit under authority. These questions are not hypothetical traps or spiritual interrogations. They are structured invitations for candidates to demonstrate how their values operate in real situations.

Many interviews rely heavily on affirmational questions. Candidates are asked what they believe, what they value, or how they would describe their leadership. These questions are easy to answer well and difficult to evaluate meaningfully. Alignment is rarely revealed through self-description. It is revealed through response to tension, limits, and accountability.

Effective alignment questions introduce boundaries. They clarify expectations, then observe the reaction. How does the candidate respond when authority is defined clearly? How do they react when non-negotiables are stated plainly? Do they ask clarifying questions, express respect, and demonstrate restraint, or do they resist, reframe, or minimize the importance of governance?

Scenario-based questions are particularly valuable. They place candidates in situations where values, doctrine, and authority intersect.

These questions are not about finding the correct answer. They are about observing reasoning, humility, and submission to governed standards. Patterns of deflection, overconfidence, or rigidity often emerge when scenarios challenge personal preference.

Questions that reveal alignment also allow space for disagreement. Faithful discernment does not require candidates to agree with every application, but it does require them to articulate how disagreement would be handled under authority. Will they submit, seek counsel, and operate within boundaries, or will they push for independence once entrusted with influence?

Tone matters. Alignment questions should be asked calmly and consistently, not confrontationally. The goal is not to pressure candidates into compliance, but to observe whether they are prepared to live under governance. Transparency strengthens discernment. Candidates should understand why questions are being asked and what authority the role will carry.

Faithful churches design interview questions in advance. They ensure that questions reflect values, doctrine, and authority rather than personal curiosity or relational chemistry. This preparation prevents drift and protects against bias.

Asking questions that reveal alignment transforms interviews from conversations into discernment tools. When questions are governed, answers become meaningful. When answers reveal alignment, authority can be entrusted with clarity rather than hope.

Behavioral And Situational Questions

Behavioral and situational questions are essential tools for discerning alignment because they reveal patterns rather than intentions. While belief statements and testimonies describe what a candidate affirms, behavioral and situational questions expose how those beliefs are lived under real conditions. These questions shift the interview from abstraction to application.

Behavioral questions ask candidates to describe past experiences. They focus on what the individual actually did, how decisions were made, and how authority was handled in concrete situations. Past behavior is one of the most reliable indicators of future conduct, especially when authority and pressure are involved.

Situational questions present realistic scenarios that the candidate may face if hired. These questions are not hypothetical exercises in creativity. They are designed to test judgment, restraint, and submission to governance. How a candidate responds to boundaries, conflict, and ambiguity reveals whether they are prepared to operate under authority rather than independently.

Effective behavioral questions explore moments of tension. They ask about correction, disagreement, failure, and limitation. For example, how the candidate responded when a leader overruled them, or how they handled a situation where values conflicted with outcomes. These questions surface humility, teachability, and respect for authority.

Situational questions should introduce governed constraints. Candidates should be told what values apply, what authority limits exist, and what accountability structure is in place. The goal is not to see how the candidate would redesign the system, but how they would operate faithfully within it. Resistance to constraints often signals future conflict.

These questions must be evaluated carefully. Strong candidates may acknowledge mistakes, demonstrate growth, and articulate lessons learned. Concerning patterns include blame-shifting, justification of boundary violations, or dismissal of oversight. The focus is not perfection, but posture.

Behavioral and situational questions also protect candidates. They provide clarity about expectations and authority before a role is accepted. Candidates who recognize misalignment early are spared the difficulty of discovering it after authority has been granted.

Faithful churches intentionally integrate behavioral and situational questions. They do not rely on charisma or confidence. They listen for consistency, humility, and alignment across responses. When patterns are clear, discernment becomes grounded rather than speculative.

Behavioral and situational questions turn interviews into windows. They allow leaders to see how values, doctrine, and authority operate in practice. When used wisely, they help ensure that authority is entrusted to those prepared to carry it faithfully.

Identifying Defensiveness, Ambiguity, Or Avoidance

Discernment in interviews is not limited to what is said. It includes how responses are delivered, framed, and navigated. Defensiveness, ambiguity, and avoidance are not automatic disqualifiers, but they are important signals. When authority, accountability, and values are discussed, these patterns often reveal readiness or resistance more clearly than content alone.

Defensiveness appears when questions about boundaries, correction, or authority are perceived as threats rather than stewardship. Candidates may become argumentative, overexplain, or shift responsibility. They may frame past conflicts as misunderstandings caused by others or minimize the legitimacy of oversight. While everyone desires to be understood, consistent defensiveness suggests discomfort with accountability.

Ambiguity surfaces through vague language, generalities, or spiritualized responses that avoid specificity. Candidates may speak in broad terms about calling, freedom, or grace without addressing the practical realities of authority and limits. Ambiguity often masks uncertainty or unwillingness to be examined. Alignment cannot be confirmed when answers lack clarity.

Avoidance occurs when candidates redirect questions, change topics, or offer unrelated examples rather than engaging directly. This may include excessive humor, storytelling that never resolves, or repeated reframing of the question. Avoidance can indicate fear of exposure, lack of preparation, or resistance to the authority implied by the question.

It is important to distinguish between nervousness and pattern. Many candidates experience anxiety during interviews. Single instances of hesitation or imperfect answers are normal. Concern arises when defensiveness, ambiguity, or avoidance recur across different questions and contexts. Patterns indicate posture.

Leaders should respond to these signals with calm follow-up rather than confrontation. Clarifying questions often reveal whether the issue is a misunderstanding or misalignment. Willing candidates welcome clarification and engage thoughtfully. Resistant candidates double down or disengage.

Documenting observations is essential. Impressions should be recorded and discussed collectively rather than acted upon individually. Shared discernment reduces bias and ensures that decisions are grounded in observed patterns rather than isolated reactions.

Identifying defensiveness, ambiguity, or avoidance is not about exclusion. It is about protection. These patterns often predict future difficulty with correction, boundaries, or governance. Addressing them before authority is granted preserves trust and prevents conflict that would be far more damaging later.

Faithful churches listen not only for right answers, but for right posture. When leaders learn to recognize and interpret these signals wisely, interviews become instruments of discernment rather than exercises in persuasion.

Red Flags That Should Pause A Hire

Red flags are not accusations. They indicate that discernment is incomplete and that authority should not yet be delegated. Faithful hiring does not require leaders to interpret every concern as a disqualification, but it does require them to slow down when warning signs appear. Pausing is an act of stewardship, not fear.

One of the most significant red flags is resistance to authority. This may appear subtly through dismissive language about past leaders, consistent blame-shifting, or an emphasis on independence framed as calling or conviction. Candidates who struggle to submit to authority before being hired will not suddenly become governable after authority is granted.

Another red flag is inconsistency between stated beliefs and demonstrated behavior. Candidates may articulate strong convictions while describing actions that contradict them. This includes minimizing past failures without evidence of accountability, repentance, or change. Alignment is revealed through patterns, not declarations.

Defensiveness when discussing correction, boundaries, or non-negotiables should also prompt caution. A candidate who becomes guarded, argumentative, or evasive when limits are clarified may be signaling discomfort with governance. Authority requires restraint. Resistance to restraint often predicts future conflict.

Vagueness about doctrine, values, or expectations is another concern. While not every candidate will articulate theology with precision, those entrusted with influence must demonstrate clarity where it matters. Persistent ambiguity, especially when clarification is offered, suggests either misalignment or unwillingness to engage honestly.

Reluctance toward accountability structures is a critical red flag. Candidates who resist supervision, minimize the need for evaluation, or frame accountability as mistrust are not prepared to carry authority. Accountability is not a concession. It is a requirement.

Unexamined pressure to move quickly should also be treated as a warning. When leaders feel compelled to proceed despite unresolved concerns because of need, urgency, or emotional momentum, governance is being overridden. Timing pressure often precedes regrettable decisions.

Finally, a lack of curiosity can indicate misalignment. Candidates who do not ask thoughtful questions about authority, expectations, boundaries, or accountability may not be considering the weight of the job position. Readiness for authority includes a desire for clarity, not just opportunity.

Red flags do not always mean no. They mean 'not yet' or 'not this role'. Faithful churches treat pauses as protective. They use concern as an invitation to ask better questions, seek counsel, and pray with patience.

Authority, once granted, is difficult to retract without harm. Recognizing and honoring red flags before a hire preserves trust, protects the church, and respects the individual by refusing to place them into a responsibility they may not be prepared to carry.

Chapter 12
References, Backgrounds, and Wisdom

No hiring process is complete without verification. References and background review are not acts of suspicion. They are expressions of wisdom. In the church, where authority carries spiritual weight and long-term influence, failing to confirm what has been discerned places both the congregation and the individual at risk.

References exist to reveal patterns that interviews cannot. Candidates present themselves intentionally, often sincerely, but selectively. References provide an external perspective on a character's consistency and on how authority has been exercised over time. They confirm whether what has been said aligns with what has been lived.

Wisdom requires asking the right people the right questions. Churches often accept references provided solely by the candidate and ask general questions that yield predictable praise. Faithful discernment seeks references who have observed the candidate under authority, in conflict, and over time. This may include former supervisors, elders, peers, or accountability partners.

Background review is not about disqualifying people for past mistakes. It is about understanding context, patterns, and risk. Some histories require support and accountability rather than exclusion. Others may indicate that authority should not be entrusted, at least not in the role being considered. Wisdom distinguishes between redemption and readiness.

Churches sometimes avoid reference checks or background reviews out of discomfort or fear of appearing ungracious. This avoidance confuses grace with neglect. Grace does not remove responsibility. It applies it carefully. Scripture calls leaders to be above reproach, not above examination.

Transparency matters. Candidates should know that references and background review are part of the process and understand why. This clarity reinforces governance and allows candidates to participate honestly. Resistance to verification often signals discomfort with accountability.

Wisdom also requires restraint in interpretation. No reference is neutral. Leaders must listen for patterns rather than isolated comments and consider context rather than reacting emotionally. Shared review and discussion among leadership protects against bias and overreaction.

Faithful churches treat references and background review as confirmation, not discovery. They are not substitutes for discernment. They are safeguards that ensure alignment is maintained beyond the interview room.

This chapter reinforces a central truth of faithful hiring. Authority must be verified before it is entrusted. When churches practice wisdom through disciplined reference and background review, they honor both the gospel and those they seek to serve by refusing to gamble with trust.

Why References Often Lie

References often lie, not because people are malicious, but because the system encourages distortion. In church hiring, references are frequently shaped by loyalty, conflict avoidance, fear of liability, or a desire to be gracious. The result is information that is incomplete, sanitized, or misleading, even when everyone involved believes they are acting in good faith.

One common reason references lie is relational pressure. Former supervisors, pastors, or peers may feel responsible for the candidate's future and hesitate to share concerns that could hinder an opportunity. In church culture, honesty is often confused with unkindness. As a result, difficult truths are softened or omitted entirely.

Another factor is self-protection. Organizations and leaders fear legal exposure, reputational harm, or relational fallout. References may limit their responses to safe affirmations or vague encouragement. Silence becomes the preferred form of risk management. This does not serve the hiring church or the candidate, but it is common.

References also lie through selective memory. People remember success more easily than strain, and public effectiveness more readily than private difficulty. Over time, unresolved issues are reframed as growing pains or personality differences. When asked general questions, references default to positive summaries rather than specific patterns.

Church references are especially vulnerable to this problem because of shared language. Words such as faithful, called, gifted, or relational may sound meaningful but reveal little. Without disciplined questioning, references can affirm spiritual identity without addressing governance, accountability, or behavior under authority.

Sometimes references lie because they were never close enough to know. A reference may speak honestly, even with limited exposure, unaware of deeper issues that only surfaced under pressure. In these cases, the problem is not deception, but scope. Limited observation produces limited insight.

Faithful churches must therefore approach references with wisdom rather than assumption. References should not be treated as endorsements, but as data points. Specific questions matter. Asking about conflict, correction, boundaries, and authority reveals far more than asking whether someone was effective or well-liked.

This reality does not mean references are useless. It means they must be interpreted carefully. Patterns across multiple references carry weight. Vague praise repeated consistently is less informative than concrete examples offered thoughtfully.

Understanding why references often lie protects churches from false confidence. It also protects candidates from being placed into roles based on incomplete truth. Wisdom does not assume dishonesty. It accounts for human limitations and designs processes accordingly.

Faithful hiring acknowledges this reality and responds with discipline rather than cynicism. When references are gathered intentionally and interpreted collectively, they become tools of confirmation rather than sources of false assurance.

How To Ask Better Questions

Better questions do not seek affirmation. They seek clarity. In church hiring, the goal of asking questions is not to confirm likability, calling, or competence. It is to discern alignment, character, and readiness for authority. This requires questions that are intentional, specific, and difficult to answer without revealing patterns.

Better questions are concrete. General questions invite general answers. Asking whether someone is faithful, gifted, or easy to work with produces predictable responses that reveal little. Specific questions require recollection, reflection, and honesty. They ask for examples, decisions, and outcomes rather than impressions.

Effective questions focus on authority and accountability. They explore how the individual has operated under oversight, how correction was received, and how boundaries were handled. For example, asking how someone responded when their judgment was overruled reveals far more than asking how they feel about teamwork. Authority exposes posture.

Better questions also introduce tension. They do not avoid difficult areas such as conflict, failure, or limitation. These questions are not accusatory. They are realistic. Leaders are shaped in moments of pressure, not in moments of comfort. Asking how someone handled disagreement, loss of trust, or enforced boundaries surfaces maturity and self-awareness.

Silence is a tool. After asking a question, leaders should resist the urge to rescue the conversation. Pauses allow individuals to think, clarify, or reveal discomfort. Over-explaining or quickly reframing a question often prevents an honest response. Patience creates space for truth.

Follow-up questions matter. When answers are vague or overly polished, request clarification calmly. Asking for specifics, timelines, or outcomes helps distinguish between narrative and reality. Willingness to clarify is often more revealing than the clarification itself.

Better questions are consistent across candidates. This protects against bias and emotional drift. When everyone is asked the same core questions, discernment is grounded in comparison rather than impression. Deviations can be explored, but the standard remains shared.

Tone is critical. Questions should be asked respectfully and without an agenda. The goal is not to corner or expose, but to understand. Candidates should know why questions are being asked and how their answers will be used. Transparency strengthens trust even when alignment is not confirmed.

Finally, better questions are documented and discussed collectively. Individual impressions are unreliable. Shared reflection allows patterns to emerge and prevents one voice from dominating discernment. Wisdom is exercised in community, not isolation.

Asking better questions does not guarantee perfect decisions. It does, however, reduce risk and increase clarity. When churches commit to disciplined questioning, they move from hopeful hiring to faithful stewardship, treating authority with the seriousness it deserves.

Legal And Ethical Guardrails

Faithful church hiring must be both spiritually responsible and legally sound. Legal and ethical guardrails are not secular intrusions into sacred work. They are protections that preserve integrity, prevent harm, and ensure that discernment is exercised without violating trust, dignity, or law. Ignoring these guardrails does not increase faithfulness. It exposes the church and the individual to unnecessary risk.

Legal guardrails establish boundaries around what may be asked, recorded, and acted upon during the hiring process. Churches must understand applicable employment laws, including nondiscrimination requirements, privacy protections, and proper use of background information. Even when spiritual qualification is essential, questions must be framed carefully and consistently to avoid unlawful bias or improper inquiry.

Ethical guardrails go beyond legal minimums. They govern how information is gathered, interpreted, and used. Leaders must resist curiosity that exceeds authority. Not every personal detail is relevant to a role's readiness. Ethical discernment distinguishes between information that protects the church and intrusion that violates trust.

Transparency is a core ethical requirement. Candidates should know what the process includes, what information will be reviewed, and how decisions will be made. Hidden criteria or undisclosed concerns undermine fairness and damage credibility. Ethical processes treat candidates with respect regardless of outcome.

Confidentiality is also critical. Information shared during interviews, references, or background reviews must be handled with restraint. Gossip masquerading as discernment harms witnesses and individuals unnecessarily. Access to sensitive information should be limited to those with clear authority and responsibility.

Consistency protects against both legal exposure and ethical drift. When standards are applied unevenly or exceptions are made quietly, accountability collapses. Ethical hiring requires that values, questions, and criteria be applied uniformly, even when doing so slows the process or costs convenience.

Churches must also guard against spiritual coercion. Candidates should never feel pressured to disclose more than is appropriate or to conform superficially to be accepted. Discernment invites honesty. It does not demand performance.

Legal and ethical guardrails do not hinder spiritual discernment. They discipline it. They ensure that authority is exercised justly, that decisions are defensible, and that people are treated as image bearers rather than as means to an end.

Faithful churches understand that governance includes restraint. When hiring processes honor legal requirements and ethical responsibility, discernment remains credible, authority is protected, and the church's witness is strengthened rather than compromised.

Discernment Questions for the Interview and Evaluation Process

The questions at the conclusion of Part IV are designed to evaluate the process itself, not merely the candidate. They help ensure that discernment remains disciplined, shared, and governed rather than rushed, subjective, or emotionally driven. These questions should be asked repeatedly throughout the interview process by the hiring authority.

Questions for Leadership During the Discernment Process

• Have we defined the purpose of each interview stage, and are we honoring those boundaries?

• Are we allowing adequate time between interviews for reflection, prayer, and discussion?

• Are decisions being influenced by urgency, relief, or emotional momentum rather than clarity?

• Have concerns been surfaced and discussed openly, or quietly dismissed for the sake of progress?

• Are we relying on shared criteria or individual impressions to guide discernment?

• Have all voices with appropriate authority been heard before advancing the process?

Questions That Test the Quality of the Interview Process

• Are our questions revealing posture and patterns, or merely confirming information already known?

• Are candidates given clear information about authority, boundaries, and accountability?

• Are we observing how candidates respond to limits and corrections during the interview itself?

• Have we asked consistent core questions across candidates to prevent bias?

• Are we documenting observations and patterns rather than relying on memory or feeling?

Questions for Interpreting Discernment Signals

• Are we paying attention to defensiveness, ambiguity, or avoidance, or explaining them away?

• Are we distinguishing nervousness from repeated patterns of resistance?

• Are we allowing follow-up questions to clarify concerns, or moving forward prematurely?

• Are we weighing patterns across interviews, references, and interactions rather than isolated moments?

Questions Before Making a Final Decision

• Has alignment been confirmed, or are we hoping it will develop after hiring?

• Are all non-negotiables clearly affirmed and demonstrated, not just verbally accepted?

• Have references and background information confirmed rather than contradicted what we observed?

• Are we prepared to explain and defend this decision based on values and governance, not sentiment?

• If authority must later be corrected or withdrawn, will we have clarity to act justly?

How These Questions Should Be Used

These questions are not a checklist to rush through at the end of the process. They are safeguards to be revisited as discernment unfolds. When uncertainty remains, delay is appropriate. When alignment is clear, confidence is justified.

Part IV reinforces a central discipline. Discernment must be structured, shared, and governed. When the interview process itself is evaluated honestly, hiring decisions become faithful acts of stewardship rather than hopeful leaps of faith.

Part V
Employment, Compensation, and Stewardship

Hiring does not end with discernment. When a church extends an offer of employment, it enters into a stewardship relationship that carries spiritual, ethical, and practical responsibility. Compensation, benefits, expectations, and boundaries all communicate values, whether intentionally or not. How a church structures employment reveals what it truly honors and what it is willing to protect.

Many churches treat compensation and employment terms as administrative necessities rather than governance decisions. This approach creates misalignment between stated values and lived practice. When roles are spiritually weighty but structurally vague, or when expectations are high but support is inconsistent, authority is strained and trust erodes.

Employment in the church is not merely transactional. It is relational and representative. Staff members are entrusted not only with tasks, but with time, livelihood, and influence. Stewardship requires clarity, fairness, and restraint. Churches must resist the temptation to spiritualize sacrifice in ways that excuse poor structure or inequitable treatment.

This section addresses how employment terms should reflect values governance. It explores compensation as stewardship rather than reward, the importance of clear expectations and boundaries, and the ethical responsibilities that accompany authority. It also addresses common failures, such as role creep, unpaid labor expectations, and compensation decisions driven by budget pressure rather than discernment.

Faithful churches recognize that stewardship applies to people as much as to resources. Employment decisions must honor dignity, sustainability, and accountability. When compensation and expectations are governed clearly, staff members are protected from burnout and resentment, and the church is protected from instability and conflict.

Part V moves the hiring process into long-term responsibility. Authority has been entrusted. Alignment has been confirmed. The question now is whether the church will steward that authority with integrity through fair employment practices and disciplined governance.

Chapter 13 Compensation Communicates Values

Compensation is not a secondary concern or a purely administrative decision. It is a theological and governance statement. How a church compensates its staff reveals what it values, how it understands stewardship, and whether it is willing to align its beliefs with its practices. Compensation communicates worth, expectation, and responsibility, whether intentionally designed or quietly assumed.

In many churches, compensation is shaped more by budget pressure than by discernment. Roles expand while pay remains static. Expectations increase without corresponding support. Sacrifice is spiritualized in ways that excuse imbalance. Over time, this creates resentment, burnout, and quiet disengagement. What begins as faith-driven service erodes into survival.

Faithful compensation begins with honesty. Churches must acknowledge that staff members exchange their time, skills, and energy for a livelihood. While ministry is a calling, employment is still employment. Confusing the two allows churches to benefit from labor without fully accounting for its cost. Stewardship requires clarity, not guilt-driven generosity or vague gratitude.

Compensation must align with the role, authority, and responsibilities. Roles that carry greater authority, influence, or risk require greater care in compensation design. Paying a role as support while expecting leadership-level responsibility creates misalignment. Authority without adequate provision places unfair strain on both the individual and their family.

Fair compensation also protects governance. When staff members are underpaid, financial stress quietly influences decision-making, availability, and a posture toward leadership. Dependence increases vulnerability. Silence replaces honesty. Correction becomes harder when livelihood feels threatened. Adequate compensation creates freedom for accountability rather than fear.

Churches often justify inadequate compensation by appealing to spiritual reward or future provision. Scripture does not support this practice. Faithfulness does not excuse neglect. Stewardship calls leaders to provide responsibly for those who labor among them, not to test their endurance or commitment through financial strain.

Compensation decisions must also be consistent. Disparities that cannot be explained by role, responsibility, or experience undermine trust. Quiet exceptions and informal adjustments create confusion and resentment. Transparency, even when resources are limited, strengthens credibility.

This chapter does not prescribe salary ranges or formulas. What it insists upon is alignment. Compensation must reflect values, authority, and responsibility honestly. It must be discussed openly, reviewed regularly, and adjusted with care.

Faithful churches do not treat compensation as an afterthought. They recognize it as an extension of governance and stewardship. When compensation is aligned with authority and values, staff members are supported rather than strained, accountability is strengthened rather than avoided, and the church's witness is preserved through integrity rather than explanation.

Fair Pay And Honest Expectations

Fair pay and honest expectations must go hand in hand. One without the other creates imbalance and undermines stewardship. When churches expect more than they are willing to support or compensate without clearly defining expectations, authority becomes strained, and trust erodes quietly over time.

Fair pay begins with realism. Churches must assess what role they are asking a person to carry, not what they hope it will become. Authority, responsibility, availability, emotional labor, and risk all factor into fair compensation. When expectations resemble full-time leadership, but compensation reflects part-time support, misalignment is already present. Over time, this gap produces frustration, fatigue, and moral tension.

Honest expectations require clarity at the outset. Roles must be defined with precision, including scope, hours, availability, and boundaries. Vague language, such as 'flexible,' 'team-oriented,' or 'willing to do whatever is needed,' often masks an expectation of unlimited commitment. This ambiguity puts pressure on staff members to overextend, leaving leaders unsure what is fair to require.

Fair pay also protects against spiritual manipulation. Churches sometimes appeal to a sense of calling, sacrifice, or loyalty to justify expectations that would be considered unreasonable in any other context. While ministry involves sacrifice, stewardship requires restraint. Calling does not negate the need for sustainability. Expecting ongoing sacrifice without provision is not faithfulness. It is avoidance.

Honest expectations include what the role does not require. Clear limits protect staff members from role creep and prevent leaders from relying on goodwill rather than governance. When expectations change, compensation and authority must be revisited. Growth without recalibration is not stewardship. It is neglect.

Alignment between pay and expectations strengthens accountability. Staff members can receive corrections without fear when their livelihoods are not constantly threatened. Leaders can address issues without guilt when expectations are clear, and support is adequate. Trust grows when compensation and responsibility move together.

Fair pay does not require abundance. It requires integrity. Churches may face financial constraints, but honesty about those constraints is essential. Clear communication allows staff members to make informed decisions and prevents resentment born from unspoken assumptions.

Faithful churches treat compensation and expectations as inseparable. They define roles honestly, compensate responsibly, and revisit both regularly. When pay reflects responsibility and expectations are clear, employment becomes a sustainable expression of stewardship rather than a quiet source of strain.

Faith Language Misuse

Faith language is powerful. It shapes expectations, frames sacrifice, and signals spiritual seriousness. When used carefully, it encourages trust and obedience. When misused, it becomes a tool for avoidance, pressure, or control. In the context of employment and compensation, misuse of faith language quietly undermines stewardship and damages trust.

One common misuse is spiritualizing unmet obligations. Phrases such as "we are trusting God," "this is a season," or "we are stepping out in faith" are sometimes used to delay clarity around pay, hours, or role scope. While faith involves trust, it does not excuse failure to define expectations or provide support. Trusting God does not replace responsible leadership.

Another misuse occurs when sacrifice is assumed rather than chosen. Staff members may be told that the ministry requires giving more, staying later, or accepting less because the work is spiritual. Over time, this expectation becomes normalized. What began as a voluntary sacrifice becomes an unspoken obligation. Faith language is then used to discourage questions or recalibration, framing concern as a lack of commitment.

Faith language is also misused when calling is leveraged to justify imbalance. Individuals may be reminded of their calling when raising concerns about sustainability, compensation, or boundaries. This conflates obedience to God with compliance to circumstances. Calling does not negate limits. It requires stewardship to endure.

Churches sometimes use faith language to mask uncertainty or indecision. Rather than acknowledging budget constraints, unclear priorities, or governance gaps, leaders defer to spiritual phrasing that sounds humble but avoids responsibility. This creates confusion and erodes confidence. Staff members sense when faith language is substituting for clarity.

Misuse of faith language also affects accountability. Correction may be framed spiritually, while structural issues go unaddressed. Staff members are encouraged to pray through the strain rather than have their expectations adjusted. Over time, this creates a culture where endurance is valued more than integrity and silence is rewarded over honesty.

Faithful use of faith language aligns words with action. It pairs trust with transparency, sacrifice with consent, and calling with care. It acknowledges limits and names reality without diminishing hope. True faith does not fear clarity. It is strengthened by it.

Stewardship requires disciplined language. Churches must be careful not to use spiritual vocabulary to excuse imbalance, delay correction, or pressure compliance. When faith language is governed by values and matched with responsible action, it builds trust and sustains service. When misused, it erodes quietly and deeply.

Faith language should illuminate responsibility, not obscure it. When words and practices align, the church honors God, protects its people, and preserves its witness through integrity rather than explanation.

Bi-Vocational Clarity

Bi-vocational ministry is a legitimate and often faithful expression of service, but it requires exceptional clarity. When roles are intentionally bi-vocational, expectations, authority, compensation, and availability must be defined with precision. Without clarity, bi-vocational arrangements become a source of confusion, strain, and quiet resentment rather than a sustainable model of stewardship.

Bi-vocational clarity begins with honesty about scope. Churches must distinguish between a role that is truly part-time and one that is functionally full-time but financially unsupported. When leadership-level authority, availability, and responsibility are expected while compensation reflects limited hours, misalignment is already present. Calling cannot compensate for structural inconsistency.

Availability must be governed explicitly. Bi-vocational staff members have competing responsibilities and limited capacity. Expecting constant accessibility or rapid response outside agreed-upon hours undermines both the role and the individual's other obligations. Clear boundaries protect the church from unrealistic dependence and protect the staff member from burnout and guilt-driven overextension.

Authority must also be calibrated carefully. Bi-vocational roles often carry meaningful influence, especially in teaching, leadership, or pastoral care. That authority must be matched with realistic expectations for preparation, presence, and follow-through. Granting authority without adequate time to steward it puts integrity and quality under pressure.

Compensation in bi-vocational roles must be framed accurately. Pay should reflect the actual scope of work, not aspirational hopes. If a role is expected to grow, that growth must be planned, reviewed, and adjusted formally rather than assumed. Growth without recalibration is not faith. It is neglect.

Clarity also requires protecting the role from mission creep. Bi-vocational staff are often willing and capable, which makes them vulnerable to the gradual expansion of their responsibilities. Without explicit limits, willingness becomes expectation. Clear role definitions and regular review are essential safeguards.

Faithful bi-vocational arrangements honor transparency and consent. Individuals must understand the demands, limitations, and tradeoffs of the role before accepting it. Churches must respect those limits after the role begins. This mutual clarity preserves trust and sustainability.

Bivocational ministry can be a gift to the church when wisely governed. It allows flexibility, shared leadership, and broader participation. When governed poorly, it becomes a quiet source of strain that harms both the church and the individual serving.

Stewardship requires naming reality. Bi-vocational clarity ensures that authority, expectations, and compensation move together. When they do, service is sustainable, accountability is fair, and faithfulness is protected over time.

Chapter 14
Employment Structures Churches Misunderstand

Churches often inherit employment practices without examining whether they are appropriate, ethical, or sustainable. Titles, classifications, and arrangements are adopted from tradition, convenience, or assumption rather than governance. When employment structures are misunderstood, authority becomes blurred, accountability weakens, and both the church and the individual are exposed to unnecessary risk.

One common misunderstanding involves treating spiritual roles as exempt from normal employment clarity. Churches may assume that because work is ministry, formal structure is unnecessary. This assumption leads to vague agreements, inconsistent expectations, and informal enforcement. Ministry does not eliminate the need for structure. It increases it.

Another frequent error is confusing spiritual authority with employment authority. A staff member may be spiritually influential but lack organizational authority, or vice versa. When these distinctions are not made explicit, correction becomes confused. Leaders may hesitate to address performance issues because they feel they are challenging calls rather than employment expectations. Governance collapses when authority categories are conflated.

Churches also misunderstand the implications of employee-versus-contractor arrangements. Independent contractors are often used to reduce costs or administrative burdens, but they are not employees. They cannot be governed in the same way, expected to follow internal policies, or subjected to the same level of control. Treating contractors like employees creates legal and ethical problems that can damage trust and expose the church to liability.

Volunteer roles are another area of confusion. Volunteers may carry significant influence without clear accountability because they are not paid. Payment status, however, does not determine authority. Influence does. When volunteers teach, lead, or discipline without defined governance, authority is exercised without structure. This creates a risk equal to, and sometimes greater than, that of paid roles.

Churches also struggle with hybrid roles that shift over time. A volunteer becomes part-time staff. A part-time role expands into full-time responsibility. Compensation, authority, and expectations lag behind reality. Without formal recalibration, these roles operate in constant misalignment. What was once generous becomes exploitative, often unintentionally.

Titles can further obscure structure. Words like pastor, director, coordinator, or minister are used inconsistently, sometimes to honor service and other times to justify authority. Titles without defined authority confuse staff, congregants, and external partners. Authority should be defined by role and responsibility, not by title alone.

Faithful governance requires an intentional employment structure. Churches must know who is an employee, who is a contractor, who is a volunteer, and what authority each role legitimately carries. These distinctions are not bureaucratic. They are protective.

Understanding employment structures allows churches to steward people responsibly. It ensures expectations are fair, authority is legitimate, and accountability is enforceable. When employment structures are misunderstood, even well-meaning churches drift into inconsistency and harm. When they are clarified, leadership becomes stable, trust is preserved, and stewardship is practiced with integrity rather than assumption.

Employee Vs. Contractor

Churches often misunderstand the distinction between employees and contractors, treating the difference as administrative rather than governance-related. This misunderstanding creates legal exposure, ethical inconsistencies, and confusion about authority. Employee and contractor classifications are not interchangeable. Each carries different expectations, rights, and limits that must be respected if stewardship is to be practiced faithfully.

Employees operate under the authority of the organization. They are directed in how, when, and where work is performed. Employees are subject to internal policies, supervision, performance evaluations, and corrective action. Because employees function under organizational control, the church bears responsibility for their conduct, compensation structure, and working conditions. Authority and accountability are inherent in the relationship.

Contractors, by contrast, are independent providers of defined services. They control how the work is performed and are engaged for specific outcomes rather than ongoing oversight. Contractors are not subject to the same internal policies as employees. They are accountable for results, not submission to organizational authority. Treating contractors as employees undermines the legitimacy of the arrangement and exposes the church to legal and ethical risk.

Problems arise when churches expect contractor-level cost savings while demanding employee-level compliance. Contractors may be required to attend staff meetings, follow internal ministry procedures, submit to supervision, or be available beyond the scope of their agreement. These expectations contradict the nature of a contractor relationship and blur authority boundaries. Over time, this inconsistency becomes unsustainable.

The misuse of contractor classification is often driven by budget pressure or convenience rather than discernment. Churches may rationalize misclassification by appealing to spiritual calling or mutual trust. These justifications do not change the reality of the relationship.

Faithfulness does not override responsibility. Stewardship requires alignment between classification and practice.

Authority must match structure. If a role requires ongoing direction, integration into leadership teams, and submission to internal governance, it is an employee role. If a role requires independence, limited scope, and outcome-based engagement, it is a contractor role. Attempting to combine the two undermines accountability on both sides.

Transparency is essential. Individuals must understand the nature of the relationship before accepting the role. Expectations, limits, compensation structure, and authority must be stated clearly. Surprises erode trust and create moral tension, even when intentions are sincere.

Faithful churches do not use classification to avoid responsibility. They choose structures that reflect reality. When employee and contractor roles are defined and honored properly, authority is exercised legitimately, accountability is enforceable, and both the church and the individual are protected.

Stewardship requires structural honesty. Employment classifications are not technicalities. They are governance decisions. When churches align authority, expectations, and classification, they preserve integrity, protect witness, and practice leadership with clarity rather than assumption.

Pastoral Housing Allowances

Pastoral housing allowances are a legitimate provision within church employment, but they are frequently misunderstood, misapplied, or poorly governed. When handled carelessly, they create confusion, inequity, and risk. When handled wisely, they serve as tools of stewardship that support pastoral sustainability without distorting authority or accountability.

A housing allowance is not a bonus, a perk, or discretionary generosity. It is a structured component of compensation intended to support pastors whose work requires stability, availability, and presence within the life of the church. Because it affects both compensation structure and tax treatment, it must be approached with clarity and restraint.

One common failure is treating the housing allowance informally. Churches may retroactively designate allowances, inconsistently adjust amounts, or fail to document their decisions properly. This lack of discipline exposes both the church and the pastor to legal and financial risk. Stewardship requires that housing allowances be established intentionally, approved appropriately, and documented clearly before they are applied.

Another misunderstanding occurs when housing allowances are used to mask a compensation imbalance. Churches may offer a housing allowance in place of an adequate salary, framing it as generosity while leaving overall compensation insufficient. This practice shifts the burden rather than alleviating it. A housing allowance should complement fair compensation, not compensate for its absence.

Equity and consistency also matter. Housing allowances should be tied to role, authority, and responsibility rather than negotiated privately or adjusted arbitrarily. Quiet exceptions undermine trust and create confusion among staff. Transparent processes protect both leadership and pastors from resentment and misunderstanding.

Pastors must also understand the responsibility that accompanies a housing allowance. Proper use, record keeping, and compliance are personal obligations. Churches should not assume knowledge or leave pastors to navigate these requirements unsupported. Stewardship includes education and clarity, not silence.

Housing allowances should never be used to increase leverage over a pastor. When housing support becomes a point of control or fear, authority is distorted, and trust is damaged. Compensation structures should foster accountability, not dependency that discourages honesty.

Faithful churches treat pastoral housing allowances as part of a larger employment structure governed by values, transparency, and care. They ensure that allowances are lawful, documented, equitable, and aligned with the role's authority and responsibility.

When housing allowances are handled with wisdom, they support stability rather than strain. They reflect care rather than control. And they reinforce the central principle of stewardship that runs throughout this guide. Employment structures should protect people, preserve integrity, and honor the weight of authority entrusted within the life of the church.

Benefits And Sabbaticals

Benefits and sabbaticals are not luxuries. They are expressions of stewardship and long-term wisdom. When churches neglect these provisions, they often do so unintentionally, assuming that spiritual calling will compensate for physical, emotional, and relational strain. Over time, this assumption weakens leaders, destabilizes families, and harms the church's witness.

Benefits of communicating care in tangible form. Health insurance, retirement contributions, paid leave, and disability coverage acknowledge that the ministry does not exempt individuals from ordinary human vulnerability. When churches fail to provide reasonable benefits, they transfer risk onto staff members and their families. This creates anxiety, limits transparency, and discourages honest communication about health, fatigue, or future planning.

In many churches, benefits are treated as optional or deferred until growth occurs. This approach misunderstands stewardship. Sustainability should be built into employment structures from the beginning, even when resources are limited. Clarity about what is provided and what is not allows staff members to make informed decisions and prevents resentment born from unspoken expectations.

Sabbaticals serve a different but equally important purpose. They recognize that long-term spiritual leadership requires seasons of rest, reflection, and renewal. Sabbaticals are not rewards for endurance or compensation for burnout. They are preventative measures that protect leaders from exhaustion and preserve clarity, humility, and effectiveness over time.

Churches often resist sabbaticals out of fear. They worry about continuity, cost, or dependence on a single leader. These concerns reveal deeper governance issues. A healthy church should be able to function without one individual for a defined period. Sabbaticals expose fragility where it exists and encourage shared leadership rather than personality-centered dependence.

Sabbaticals must be governed intentionally. Clear eligibility criteria, duration, expectations, and reintegration plans are essential. Without structure, sabbaticals become irregular favors or sources of resentment. With structure, they become predictable rhythms that benefit both the individual and the church.

Benefits and sabbaticals also strengthen accountability. Leaders who are supported are more likely to receive correction honestly and serve without fear. When livelihood and rest are precarious, authority becomes distorted. Silence replaces transparency, and endurance is mistaken for faithfulness.

Faithful churches view benefits and sabbaticals as investments, not expenses. They protect the long-term health of leaders and the organization's stability. They reflect a values-driven commitment to stewardship rather than short-term survival.

When benefits and sabbaticals are governed with clarity and fairness, employment becomes sustainable rather than sacrificial. Leaders are cared for, families are protected, and the church honors God not only through what it teaches, but through how it treats those entrusted with authority.

Stewardship Questions for Employment, Compensation, and Care

Leadership teams should ask these questions before extending offers and revisit them regularly after employment begins.
They are stewardship questions, not negotiation tools.

Questions for Church Leadership Before Extending an Offer

- Does this compensation accurately reflect the authority, responsibility, and availability required by the role?
- Are expectations clearly defined, or are we relying on goodwill and sacrifice to fill gaps?
- Have we separated calling from employment so that faith language is not masking an imbalance?
- Are we asking this individual to live under conditions we would not accept ourselves?
- If expectations increase, have we committed to revisiting compensation and authority formally?

Questions That Test Structural Integrity

- Is this role properly classified as employee, contractor, or volunteer based on actual expectations?
- Are authority and accountability aligned with the employment structure we are using?
- Are compensation decisions documented, approved, and applied consistently?
- Would this structure withstand outside scrutiny if examined carefully?
- Are we using informal arrangements to avoid responsibility rather than steward it?

Questions About Sustainability and Care

• Does this role allow for rest, health, and family stability over time?
• Have benefits, leave, and sabbatical expectations been clearly communicated?
• Are we protecting staff from burnout, or quietly normalizing it?
• Have we created dependency through compensation structures that discourage honesty?
• Are we prepared to support this individual in seasons of strain rather than spiritualizing endurance?

Questions for Ongoing Review After Hiring

• Do current expectations still match compensation and authority?
• Have roles expanded without recalibration?
• Are faith-based appeals being used to avoid difficult employment conversations?
• Are we addressing issues early, or allowing strain to accumulate?
• Does our employment practice strengthen trust or quietly erode it?

How These Questions Should Be Used

These questions are not meant to create hesitation. They are meant to create alignment. If clarity is lacking, delay is appropriate. If misalignment exists, adjustment is required.

Part V reinforces a governing principle. Stewardship applies to people as much as to resources. When churches align employment practices with values and authority, they protect dignity, sustain service, and preserve witnesses through integrity rather than explanation.

Part VI
Onboarding, Oversight, and Protection

Hiring does not conclude when an offer is accepted. Authority has been entrusted, but it has not yet been stabilized. The earliest months of employment are where alignment is either reinforced or quietly eroded. Onboarding, oversight, and protection are not administrative follow-ups. They are governance responsibilities that determine whether authority is exercised faithfully or allowed to drift.

Many churches assume that discernment is complete once a decision is made. As a result, onboarding is rushed, expectations are implied rather than clarified, and oversight is informal. New staff members are left to infer values, boundaries, and authority through observation rather than instruction. This approach places unnecessary strain on relationships and increases the likelihood of early misalignment.

Onboarding is the moment when governance becomes operational. Values are translated into daily practice. Authority boundaries are named. Accountability pathways are established. When onboarding is intentional, staff members know how decisions are made, how concerns are raised, and how corrections are handled. When it is neglected, informal authority fills the gap.

Oversight must be active, not assumed. Leaders often hesitate to supervise closely early on, fearing they may appear distrustful. In reality, early oversight communicates care and clarity. It provides space for questions, correction, and adjustment before habits form. Oversight protects both the church and the individual by addressing issues while they are still small and relationally manageable.

Protection flows in both directions. Churches must protect doctrine, culture, and trust by consistently enforcing values. They must also protect staff members from unclear expectations, shifting standards, and unmanaged pressure. Governance that corrects without supporting, or supports without correcting, fails in its responsibility.

This section addresses how churches can onboard intentionally, establish healthy oversight rhythms, and create protective structures that sustain alignment over time. It explores supervision, evaluation, early correction, and the role of documentation in preserving clarity and fairness.

Part VI moves the hiring process into lived practice. Authority has been entrusted. Stewardship now requires consistency. Faithful churches do not assume alignment will hold. They reinforce it through disciplined onboarding, thoughtful oversight, and protective governance that honors both the role and the person serving within it.

Chapter 15
The First Year Matters More Than the Hire

Most hiring failures are not the result of poor discernment. They are the result of neglected oversight. Churches invest significant time and prayer into selecting the right person, only to assume that alignment will sustain itself once the role begins. This assumption is costly. The first year of employment shapes patterns, expectations, and authority more than the hire itself.

During the first year, informal norms are established. Staff members learn what is actually enforced, not what was discussed during interviews. Values are tested under real pressure. Authority boundaries either solidify or blur. When oversight is absent, assumptions replace clarity, and misalignment becomes embedded rather than corrected.

Early months require intentional leadership presence. New staff members need clarity on decision-making, communication pathways, and accountability. Without this guidance, individuals fill gaps based on previous experience or personal preference. Over time, these practices become habits that are difficult to reverse without relational cost.

Correction is most effective early. When issues are addressed quickly and clearly, they feel instructional rather than disciplinary. When concerns are delayed, they accumulate emotional weight and resistance. Early correction communicates care and commitment to shared standards. Delayed correction feels arbitrary and unfair.

The first year is also when trust is formed. Staff members assess whether leadership follows through on its stated values, supports them under pressure, and consistently addresses issues. Congregants observe how authority is exercised and enforced. Trust established early sustains the relationship in the long term. Trust undermined early is difficult to restore.

Churches sometimes avoid oversight during the first year out of a desire to be gracious or patient. This avoidance misinterprets grace. Grace does not remove standards. It applies them clearly and compassionately. Faithful oversight provides stability, not suspicion.

Intentional rhythms matter. Regular check-ins, documented expectations, and structured feedback create space for alignment and growth. These rhythms should be designed before the role begins and maintained consistently. Oversight should be expected, not exceptional.

The first year also protects leaders. Clear oversight allows concerns to be raised without fear and successes to be recognized without ambiguity. Staff members who know how they are evaluated are more likely to serve openly and to receive honest feedback.

Faithful churches understand that hiring is only the beginning. The first year determines whether authority is stewarded or squandered. When onboarding and oversight are intentional, alignment is reinforced, trust is built, and the church is protected from avoidable conflict long after the excitement of the hire has passed.

Onboarding As Cultural Installation

Onboarding is not orientation. It is a cultural installation. The earliest weeks of employment determine how values are interpreted, how authority is exercised, and how faithfulness is measured in practice. What is explained, modeled, and enforced during onboarding becomes the operational culture long before it is ever named.

Many churches treat onboarding as a transfer of information rather than a transfer of authority. New staff members are shown systems, schedules, and expectations, but not governance. Values are mentioned abstractly, if at all. As a result, individuals learn culture by observing what is tolerated rather than what is taught. Informal norms replace articulated standards.

Cultural installation requires intentionality. Values must be translated into daily decisions, relational boundaries, and behavioral expectations. New staff members should understand how conflict is addressed, how decisions are made, and how Scripture guides correction. Without this clarity, people rely on personal history or previous church experience to fill the gaps.

Authority must be installed, not assumed. Onboarding should clarify who supervises whom, how accountability functions, and where final authority rests. When these lines are unclear, staff members either overstep or hesitate. Both outcomes create instability.

Modeling matters as much as instruction. New staff members watch how leaders handle disagreement, stress, and correction. Inconsistency between stated values and observed behavior erodes trust quickly. Cultural installation requires alignment between language and practice.

Onboarding should also create safety. Clear expectations reduce anxiety and allow staff members to ask questions without fear. When governance is explained upfront, correction feels fair rather than personal. Support and accountability can coexist without tension.

Documentation strengthens installation. Written role descriptions, values statements, supervision rhythms, and evaluation criteria provide reference points that protect both the church and the staff member. A culture that exists only in memory or tradition is fragile. Documented culture can be reinforced.

Faithful onboarding is paced. It allows time for questions, reflection, and adjustment. It does not overwhelm, but it does not avoid clarity. Early investment in cultural installation prevents long-term correction.

When churches treat onboarding as cultural installation, they steward authority intentionally. Alignment becomes visible, accountability becomes predictable, and trust grows naturally. Onboarding then fulfills its purpose, not merely welcoming someone in, but installing them into a culture governed by values rather than personality or habit.

Mentoring And Supervision

Mentoring and supervision are not interchangeable. Both are essential, but they serve different purposes. When churches confuse the two, staff members either receive encouragement without accountability or oversight without support. Faithful governance requires both to be present, clearly defined, and intentionally practiced.

Supervision exists to govern authority. It clarifies expectations, evaluates performance, addresses misalignment, and enforces standards. Supervision is structured, documented, and role-based. It protects the church by ensuring that authority is exercised within agreed boundaries, and it protects staff members by making corrections predictable rather than arbitrary.

Mentoring exists to develop the person. It focuses on growth, discernment, spiritual maturity, and vocational development. Mentoring is relational rather than hierarchical. It creates space for vulnerability, questions, and reflection that may not belong in formal supervision. Mentoring supports longevity and depth rather than compliance.

Problems arise when supervision is replaced with mentoring. Leaders may avoid difficult conversations by framing all guidance as encouragement. Over time, expectations blur, correction is delayed, and accountability weakens. Staff members are left uncertain about where they stand or what is required of them.

Conversely, problems also arise when supervision lacks mentoring. Staff members receive corrections without care or evaluation, and without development. This creates fear, defensiveness, and disengagement. Authority becomes transactional rather than formative.

Staff members should know which conversations are supervisory and which are mentoring. Supervision meetings should be documented and tied to role expectations. Mentoring conversations should be confidential, supportive, and focused on growth rather than performance.

Churches must also consider who fills each role. A direct supervisor may not be the best mentor. In some cases, separating these roles allows for greater honesty and balance. Mentors should be trusted, spiritually mature, and free from evaluative power over the individual they mentor.

Regular rhythms matter. Supervision should occur consistently, not only when problems arise. Mentoring should be available but not forced. Both should be structured intentionally rather than left to chance or personality.

Faithful churches recognize that authority without care hardens people, and care without authority confuses them. When mentoring and supervision are practiced together, staff members are supported, accountability is sustained, and culture is reinforced rather than diluted.

Mentoring and supervision are not optional. They are stewardship tools. When governed well, they protect leaders, strengthen alignment, and sustain faithfulness over time.

Early Correction And Clarity

Early correction is not a sign that hiring failed. It is evidence that governance is functioning. When churches avoid correction in the early stages of employment, they often do so out of fear, misplaced grace, or discomfort with tension. This avoidance does not protect relationships. It quietly undermines them.

Clarity at the beginning establishes fairness. New staff members need to know what success looks like, how misalignment is addressed, and who has the authority to intervene. When expectations are not reinforced early, individuals assume their behavior is acceptable. Later correction then feels surprising or unjust, even when the concern is legitimate.

Early correction works because patterns are still forming. Habits are flexible. Posture is receptive. Addressing concerns early allows course correction without shame or defensiveness. The same issue addressed a year later carries emotional weight, history, and resistance that could have been avoided.

Correction must be specific. Vague feedback creates confusion and anxiety. Clear correction names the behavior, explains why it matters, and connects it to shared values or role expectations. This keeps correction principled rather than personal and reinforces governance rather than personality.

Tone matters, but clarity matters more. Gentle delivery does not compensate for unclear standards. Staff members are better served by direct, respectful correction than by silence framed as patience. Clarity builds trust by removing uncertainty.

Documentation supports clarity. Written summaries of expectations, feedback, and agreed adjustments protect both the church and the individual. Documentation is not punitive. It preserves memory, prevents drift, and ensures fairness if issues resurface. When corrections are documented early, they feel normal rather than threatening.

Churches sometimes delay correction to protect morale. In reality, unaddressed misalignment damages morale more deeply. Staff members feel inconsistent and anxious when standards are unclear or unevenly enforced. Early correction stabilizes culture by demonstrating that values are real and enforced consistently.

Clarity also protects leaders. When expectations and corrections are articulated early, leaders are less likely to personalize conflict or carry unspoken frustration. Authority can be exercised calmly and confidently rather than reactively.

Faithful churches understand that early correction is an act of care. It honors the individual by treating them as capable of alignment and growth. It honors the church by protecting culture before damage occurs.

When early correction is paired with clarity, onboarding becomes formative rather than fragile. Authority is installed, trust is strengthened, and alignment is preserved before drift becomes division.

Chapter 16
Accountability, Discipline, and Restoration

Accountability, discipline, and restoration are inseparable in faithful church governance. When any one of these is isolated or neglected, authority becomes distorted. Accountability without restoration hardens. Restoration without accountability weakens. Discipline without clarity wounds rather than heals. Faithful churches hold these realities together and practice them intentionally.

Accountability exists to protect trust. It ensures that authority is exercised within agreed boundaries and that values are enforced consistently. Without accountability, expectations become optional, and leadership becomes personality-driven. Accountability is not suspicion. It is stewardship. It clarifies who is responsible, what is required, and how concerns are addressed.

Discipline is the mechanism by which accountability is enforced. It is not punishment. It is correction with purpose. Discipline names misalignment, applies consequence where necessary, and seeks to restore order and faithfulness. When churches avoid discipline out of fear or misplaced grace, they allow harm to continue unchecked. When discipline is applied arbitrarily or emotionally, it damages credibility and deepens division.

Clarity is essential before discipline can be just. Expectations, values, and authority must be defined in advance. Discipline that enforces unstated standards or shifting expectations is unjust. Faithful discipline refers back to what was agreed upon, documented, and communicated. This protects both the church and the individual from confusion and resentment.

Restoration is the goal, not the assumption. Scripture affirms restoration, but it does not guarantee immediate reinstatement of authority. Restoration addresses relationship, posture, and faithfulness. Reinstatement addresses readiness for responsibility. Confusing the two places puts the church at risk. Some roles require extended time, accountability, or reassignment before authority can be restored responsibly.

Churches often struggle with discipline involving leaders. Fear of conflict, reputation damage, or loss of momentum leads to delay or quiet reassignment rather than clear action. This avoidance signals that authority is negotiable and values are flexible. Over time, trust erodes as congregants sense inconsistency between teaching and practice.

Discipline must be proportionate and appropriate to the role. Greater authority carries greater responsibility. Leaders entrusted with teaching, influence, or discipline are held to higher standards because the cost of misalignment is greater. This is not favoritism. It is stewardship.

Documentation matters throughout this process. Clear records of expectations, concerns, conversations, and actions protect fairness and transparency. Documentation is not about building a case. It is about preserving truth and preventing revision of history when emotions rise.

Restoration requires community and patience. It cannot be rushed to relieve discomfort or restore appearance. Genuine restoration includes repentance, change, and evidence over time. It may include counseling, supervision, or removal from certain responsibilities. These measures are not punitive. They are protective.

Faithful churches understand that accountability, discipline, and restoration are expressions of love rightly ordered. They protect the body, honor the individual, and preserve the church's witness. When these practices are governed by values and applied consistently, authority is exercised with integrity and hope rather than fear or avoidance.

This chapter affirms a difficult truth. The health of a church is revealed not in how it celebrates leaders, but in how it corrects them. Where accountability is clear, discipline is just, and restoration is patient, the church reflects the character of Christ through both truth and grace.

Biblical Discipline In Employment Contexts

Biblical discipline does not disappear when ministry becomes employment. It must be applied with greater care, not less. When churches separate spiritual discipline from employment structure, they create confusion about authority, fairness, and responsibility. Faithful governance integrates biblical discipline with clear employment processes so that correction is both just and restorative.

Scripture presents discipline as purposeful correction aimed at restoration, not punishment or control. In an employment context, this means discipline must be grounded in clearly defined expectations, articulated values, and legitimate authority. Discipline applied without prior clarity becomes arbitrary. Discipline applied without compassion becomes destructive.

Employment discipline differs from informal pastoral correction because it carries structural consequences. Roles, compensation, access, and authority may be affected. For this reason, biblical discipline in employment must be documented, proportionate, and consistent. Spiritual language cannot replace due process. Grace does not eliminate structure. It requires it.

Biblical discipline always addresses behavior and posture, not identity or calling. Correction names what is misaligned, why it matters, and what change is required. It does not shame, speculate, or spiritualize failure. When discipline shifts from correcting behavior to questioning calling or character broadly, it becomes coercive rather than corrective.

Process matters. Scripture emphasizes witnesses, clarity, and patience. In employment contexts, this translates into progressive correction where appropriate, shared oversight, and documented communication. Discipline should not be hidden or improvised. It should follow established pathways that protect both the church and the individual.

Restoration remains the goal, but restoration must be understood carefully. Restoration to fellowship does not automatically mean restoration to role. Authority may need to be temporarily limited or removed, especially in positions involving teaching, leadership, or discipline. This distinction protects the church and honors the seriousness of entrusted authority.

Churches often struggle to apply discipline consistently across roles. Volunteers, staff, and pastors may be treated differently based on visibility or perceived indispensability. Biblical discipline does not adjust standards to preserve comfort or momentum. Greater authority requires greater accountability.

Tone and posture are critical. Discipline must be exercised humbly, without anger or fear. Leaders should approach correction with a readiness to listen, clarify, and support change. Discipline delivered defensively or reactively undermines its purpose and damages trust.

Biblical discipline also requires restraint. Not every failure requires the same response. Wisdom discerns patterns, severity, and impact. Employment discipline should be appropriate to the role and the harm involved, neither minimizing serious issues nor unnecessarily escalating minor ones.

When churches integrate biblical discipline with employment governance, correction becomes credible and healing rather than confusing or threatening. Staff members know what is expected, how issues are addressed, and what restoration looks like in practice.

Biblical discipline in employment contexts reflects the character of Christ when it is clear, just, patient, and purposeful. It protects the body, honors the individual, and preserves the church's witness by demonstrating that truth and grace are not opposing forces, but disciplined companions in faithful leadership.

When Correction Becomes Termination

Termination is not the opposite of grace. In some cases, it is the final act of stewardship. When correction has been clear, authority has been exercised appropriately, and misalignment persists, termination becomes a governance decision rather than a failure of compassion. Faithful churches must be prepared to name this reality without spiritualizing avoidance or delaying responsibility.

Correction becomes termination when patterns do not change. Occasional missteps are part of growth. Repeated disregard for values, boundaries, or authority signals a deeper issue. When correction is received superficially or consistently resisted, the issue is no longer just behavior alone. It is posture. At that point, continued employment places the church, the role, and the individual at risk.

Termination must never be sudden or reactionary. It should follow documented expectations, include a clear correction, and provide a reasonable opportunity for alignment. When termination appears abrupt, it usually reflects earlier failures in clarity or courage. Faithful governance does not wait until damage is severe before acting. It addresses issues early so that outcomes, even difficult ones, are just and defensible.

Churches often hesitate to terminate because of fear. They fear conflict, reputation damage, congregational reaction, or financial strain. These fears are understandable, but they cannot govern decisions. Allowing misalignment to persist to avoid discomfort harms others. Silence becomes complicity.

Spiritual language is frequently misused at this stage. Leaders may say they are waiting on peace, praying for change, or trusting God to work things out. Prayer is essential, but it does not replace responsibility. Scripture does not require leaders to preserve roles at the expense of faithfulness. Authority exists to protect the body, not to preserve appearances.

Termination must be handled with dignity. Clear communication, respect, and appropriate support are essential. The goal is not to shame or discard, but to bring an unhealthy arrangement to an honest conclusion. Where possible, transitions should be planned carefully, with attention to confidentiality and care.

It is critical to distinguish between termination and condemnation. Ending an employment relationship does not define a person's worth, calling, or future. It acknowledges that this role, under these conditions, is no longer appropriate. Faithful leaders hold this distinction firmly and communicate it clearly.

Documentation matters greatly at this stage. Records of expectations, conversations, and corrective steps protect fairness and truth. They also protect leaders from revising history under emotional pressure. Termination should be the natural conclusion of a clear process, not a surprising event.

Congregational communication must be governed carefully. Oversharing violates dignity. Silence breeds speculation. Leaders must balance transparency with restraint, communicating what is necessary without disclosing what is private. Integrity in communication preserves trust even when decisions are painful.

When correction becomes termination, it reveals the seriousness with which a church treats authority. Avoiding termination when it is warranted weakens governance. Executing it carelessly damages witness. Performing authority faithfully demonstrates courage, clarity, and love rightly ordered.

Faithful churches understand that stewardship sometimes requires endings. When termination is handled with clarity, restraint, and compassion, it protects the body, honors the individual, and affirms that authority exists to serve truth rather than convenience.

Restoration Without Reinstatement

Restoration and reinstatement are not the same. Confusing the two is one of the most damaging errors churches make after discipling or terminating someone. Scripture calls the church to pursue restoration of relationships and spiritual health. It does not require the restoration of authority, position, or platform. Faithful governance depends on maintaining this distinction.

Restoration addresses repentance, healing, and renewed fellowship. It involves acknowledging harm, changing posture, and evidence of growth over time. Restoration is relational and spiritual. It is patient, personal, and often quiet. It seeks to repair what was broken without rushing outcomes for the sake of comfort or appearance.

Reinstatement addresses readiness for responsibility. It involves trust, accountability, and authority. Reinstatement asks whether an individual can again be entrusted with influence without placing others at risk. This question cannot be answered quickly or sentimentally. Some roles, particularly those involving teaching, leadership, or discipline, require a higher threshold for reentry.

Churches often feel pressure to reinstate quickly as proof of grace. This pressure misunderstands grace. Grace does not ignore consequences. It redeems it. Scripture consistently distinguishes forgiveness from leadership qualification. A person may be forgiven fully while remaining unqualified for a specific role, either temporarily or permanently.

Restoration without reinstatement protects both the individual and the church. It allows healing to occur without the weight of public responsibility. It prevents relapse by removing pressure to perform or prove change prematurely. It also protects congregants from confusion and potential harm.

Clear communication is essential. Individuals must understand that restoration does not guarantee a return to their role. When this distinction is not stated clearly, disappointment and resentment often follow. Faithful leaders communicate boundaries with compassion, not ambiguity.

Time matters. Restoration is observed, not declared. Consistency over time provides evidence that no statement or apology can replace. Trust is rebuilt through sustained faithfulness, not expedited processes.

Churches must also guard against quiet reinstatement. Assigning informal authority, teaching opportunities, or influence before readiness is confirmed undermines discipline and sends mixed signals. Authority should be restored intentionally or not at all.

Restoration without reinstatement is not rejection. It is stewardship. It honors the seriousness of authority and the reality of human limitation. It affirms dignity without granting access that could cause further harm.

Faithful churches practice restoration patiently and reinstatement carefully. When these are held apart, grace remains credible, accountability remains intact, and the church's witness is preserved through integrity rather than impulse.

Oversight, Accountability, and Protection Review

The questions at the conclusion of Part VI are designed to evaluate whether authority is being stewarded faithfully after hiring. They are not crisis questions. They are governance questions meant to be revisited regularly throughout a staff member's tenure.

These questions should be asked collectively by those with oversight responsibility.

Questions About Onboarding and Early Alignment

- Did onboarding clearly install values, authority boundaries, and accountability pathways?
- Were expectations documented and reinforced during the first year, or assumed?
- Did we address early misalignment promptly and clearly?
- Were supervision and mentoring roles clearly distinguished?
- Did the first year strengthen clarity or quietly normalize confusion?

Questions About Ongoing Oversight

- Is supervision occurring consistently, or only when issues arise?
- Are expectations stable, or shifting informally over time?
- Do staff members know how concerns are raised and how corrections are applied?
- Are evaluation and feedback tied to values and role definitions rather than outcomes alone?
- Is authority being exercised predictably or reactively?

Questions About Protection and Care

- Are we protecting doctrine, culture, and trust through consistent enforcement of values?
- Are we protecting staff members from unclear expectations, unmanaged pressure, or silent resentment?
- Are mentoring and support present alongside accountability?
- Have we created structures that encourage honesty rather than fear?

- Does our oversight strengthen resilience or quietly exhaust those serving?

Questions About Discipline and Restoration

- Are correction processes clear, documented, and fair?
- Do we distinguish clearly between restoration and reinstatement?
- Are disciplinary decisions governed by values or by urgency and emotion?
- Are we willing to act decisively when correction does not produce alignment?
- Would our handling of discipline withstand scrutiny if reviewed carefully?

How These Questions Should Be Used

These questions are not meant to provoke doubt. They are meant to sustain integrity. When clarity is maintained, trust grows. When oversight weakens, drift follows.

Part VI affirms a final discipline. Authority must be stewarded continuously, not assumed permanently. Faithful churches protect alignment through intentional onboarding, consistent oversight, and just accountability, preserving the health of the body and the dignity of those entrusted with leadership.

Part VII
When Hiring Goes Wrong

No hiring process is immune to failure. Even with prayer, discernment, governance, and good intentions, churches will sometimes make decisions that prove misaligned over time. The measure of faithfulness is not whether mistakes occur, but how they are addressed once they become clear. When hiring goes wrong, the response reveals whether values truly govern authority or merely decorate intention.

Many churches respond to hiring failure with denial or delay. Warning signs are minimized. Concerns are reframed as personality differences or temporary seasons. Leaders hope that time, effort, or spiritual language will resolve what clarity and courage have avoided. This approach rarely heals misalignment. It allows it to deepen.

Others respond reactively. Decisions are rushed, emotions drive action, and processes are bypassed in the name of urgency or damage control. While this may relieve immediate tension, it often creates additional harm and undermines trust. Faithful governance requires restraint even under pressure.

This section addresses what responsible leadership looks like when hiring decisions do not produce the alignment expected. It explores early recognition of misalignment, disciplined response pathways, congregational communication, and lessons that must be captured rather than ignored.

When hiring goes wrong, churches face a temptation to prioritize appearance over integrity. Leaders may fear admitting error, worrying that acknowledgment will weaken confidence or credibility. In reality, humility strengthens trust. Owning misalignment and responding with clarity demonstrates that values govern authority even when outcomes are uncomfortable.

Part VII does not exist to assign blame. It exists to restore order. It provides guidance for correcting course without compounding harm, and for ensuring that failure becomes instruction rather than precedent.

Faithful churches understand that stewardship includes repair. When hiring goes wrong, governance must become more visible, not less. Values must be enforced more clearly, not softened. Authority must be exercised with humility, not defensiveness.

This final section prepares leaders to respond when alignment fails, not with fear or avoidance, but with disciplined courage. When correction is handled faithfully, even hiring failure can become a witness to integrity, restoration, and leadership under authority rather than impulse.

Chapter 17
Common Church Hiring Failures

Most church hiring failures are not caused by bad intentions. They are caused by predictable patterns that repeat when authority is unclear, values are unenforced, and urgency replaces discernment. These failures are common precisely because they feel reasonable in the moment. Over time, they produce instability, distrust, and spiritual harm.

Hiring for Relief Rather Than Alignment

One of the most frequent failures occurs when a church hires to relieve pressure rather than confirm alignment. A role is vacant. Work is piling up. Volunteers are stretched thin. In this environment, the primary question becomes whether someone can help now, not whether they should be entrusted with authority long term. Relief-driven hiring prioritizes speed over clarity and capacity over character. The immediate pressure may ease, but misalignment is built into the decision.

Hiring for Chemistry Over Governance

Personal chemistry is powerful. Leaders feel immediate comfort with certain candidates and interpret that comfort as confirmation. Shared humor, similar backgrounds, or aligned personalities create a sense of ease that can override discipline. Governance requires more than relational comfort. When chemistry becomes the deciding factor, authority is granted without sufficient protection.

Hiring Gifting Without Boundaries

Churches often confuse visible gifting with readiness for authority. Strong communicators, musicians, organizers, or leaders may appear spiritually mature because their gifting produces results. Without clear boundaries, gifting amplifies both strengths and weaknesses. When authority is entrusted without values governance, gifting accelerates drift rather than faithfulness.

Hiring Without Defining Authority

Another common failure is hiring into undefined authority. Roles are described functionally but not governingly. Staff members are told what to do but not what authority they hold, who oversees them, or where their limits lie. In these environments, overreach and underperformance occur simultaneously. Conflict becomes personal because structure is absent.

Hiring Hope Instead of Evidence

Churches sometimes hire based on what they hope someone will become rather than on what they have consistently demonstrated. Potential is mistaken for readiness. Passion is mistaken for faithfulness. Verbal agreement is mistaken for lived alignment. When evidence is deferred until after hiring, correction becomes more costly and emotionally charged.

Hiring Without Shared Discernment

When hiring authority is concentrated in one individual without shared oversight, blind spots go unchecked. Even capable leaders miss signals when discernment is isolated. Shared processes protect against personal bias, emotional momentum, and pressure-driven decisions. Hiring without shared discernment increases the likelihood that concerns will be dismissed or unseen.

Hiring That Avoids Hard Questions

Some churches avoid difficult questions out of fear of appearing ungracious. Conflict history, accountability posture, family strain, or past discipline may be skipped entirely. Silence is mistaken for kindness. In reality, avoided questions do not disappear. They reemerge later as crises rather than conversations.

Hiring Without Post-Hire Governance

Finally, many failures occur not at the point of hire, but afterward. Onboarding is rushed. Oversight is informal. Early correction is avoided. Churches assume alignment will sustain itself. When issues surface months or years later, leaders are surprised by patterns that were never addressed early.

These failures are not mysterious. They are the natural outcome of ungoverned hiring. Each one reflects a moment when clarity was available but not exercised, when authority was delegated without protection, or when urgency displaced stewardship.

This chapter exists to normalize honesty. Recognizing these patterns allows churches to correct course without shame. When failures are clearly named, they can be consistently prevented.

Faithful churches do not deny these failures. They learn from them. When hiring mistakes are acknowledged and addressed through governance rather than justification, even failure becomes a tool for strengthening integrity, clarity, and trust.

Hiring Charisma Over Character

Charisma is compelling. It draws attention, creates momentum, and often produces immediate results. In church contexts, charisma is frequently spiritualized, interpreted as anointing, calling, or leadership presence. When charisma is mistaken for character, however, authority is granted without protection, and the consequences are often severe.

Character governs what happens when no one is watching. It shapes how authority is exercised under pressure, how truth is handled when outcomes are costly, and how people are treated when power is unchallenged. Charisma, by contrast, governs perception. It influences how someone is received, not how they will behave over time.

Churches often hire charismatic individuals because their presence promises growth, energy, or renewal. Attendance increases. Programs gain momentum. Enthusiasm spreads. These early results reinforce the decision and make concerns feel unnecessary or even disloyal. Over time, however, charisma amplifies unresolved character gaps rather than compensating for them.

One danger of charisma is that it deflects scrutiny. Charismatic leaders are often given greater freedom, fewer questions, and extended grace. Boundaries are relaxed in the name of effectiveness. Correction is delayed to avoid disrupting momentum. This creates an environment where misalignment grows unchecked.

Charisma also distorts feedback. People are less likely to confront those they admire or fear disappointing. Concerns are reframed as misunderstandings. Patterns are dismissed as isolated incidents. Over time, the cost of addressing issues feels higher than the cost of ignoring them, until harm becomes unavoidable.

Scripture consistently places character above charisma. Leadership qualifications emphasize self-control, humility, faithfulness, and integrity, not persuasiveness or presence. These standards exist because authority without character damages the body and misrepresents Christ.

Hiring charisma over character often reveals a deeper governance failure. Values are present but unenforced. Outcomes are prioritized over faithfulness. Appearance is protected at the expense of truth. These decisions are rarely made consciously, but they are predictable where values lack authority.

Faithful churches discipline themselves to look beyond initial effectiveness. They ask how a candidate handles correction, accountability, and restraint. They evaluate patterns over time rather than moments of impact. They resist the temptation to equate fruitfulness with faithfulness.

Charisma is not inherently dangerous. When governed by character and values, it can serve the church well. The danger arises when charisma is treated as evidence of readiness rather than as a trait that requires restraint.

When churches hire character over charisma, they protect authority, preserve trust, and sustain faithfulness beyond the excitement of immediate results. When they reverse this order, they may gain momentum quickly, but they will pay for it slowly and deeply.

Nepotism

Nepotism is one of the most corrosive hiring failures in the life of a church, not because family involvement is inherently wrong, but because authority becomes compromised when relationships override governance. When family ties, close friendships, or long-standing personal loyalty determine hiring decisions, values lose authority, and trust erodes quietly but deeply.

Nepotism occurs when relational proximity replaces disciplined discernment. A spouse, child, sibling, or close associate is hired not because alignment has been clearly demonstrated and governed, but because familiarity creates comfort or obligation. The decision may feel natural, even loving. Over time, it destabilizes accountability.

The primary danger of nepotism is not favoritism in opportunity, but favoritism in enforcement. When a leader hires someone they are relationally tied to, correction becomes complicated. Discipline feels personal. Oversight becomes hesitant. Boundaries soften. Even when leaders intend to remain objective, the structure itself works against fairness.

Perception matters as much as reality. Congregants and staff watch how authority is exercised. When family members or close associates receive roles, protection, or exceptions, others quickly conclude that standards are uneven. Trust declines not because people resent relationships, but because they sense that values no longer govern.

Nepotism also places unfair pressure on the individual hired. Family members are often expected to prove themselves while simultaneously benefiting from the trust assumed in them. They may receive either excessive scrutiny or excessive protection. Neither outcome is healthy. Authority exercised in the face of relational tension rarely produces clarity or confidence.

Churches sometimes defend nepotism by pointing to biblical examples of family leadership. These comparisons ignore governance context. Scripture does not excuse unaccountable authority. Family involvement in ministry still requires clear role definition, shared oversight, and enforceable accountability. Relationship does not replace qualification.

Faithful governance requires structural safeguards. When family members or close associates are considered for roles, additional transparency and shared decision-making are essential. Hiring authority should be broadened, not concentrated. Supervision should be assigned outside the relational bond whenever possible. Clear documentation protects everyone involved.

Good intentions cannot prevent nepotism. It is prevented by governance. Values must be enforced consistently regardless of the relationship. When exceptions are made quietly, authority is compromised publicly.

Churches that refuse to govern nepotism often discover its cost later. Correction becomes impossible. Conflict becomes personal. Culture fractures. What began as loyalty becomes division.

Faithful churches do not forbid relational hiring outright. They discipline it carefully. When relationships are governed rather than privileged, authority remains credible, accountability remains fair, and trust is preserved across the body.

When nepotism is confronted honestly and structured wisely, churches demonstrate that values govern leadership, not bloodlines or friendships. That clarity protects both families and congregations from harm that good intentions alone cannot prevent.

Pressure Hires

Pressure hires occur when urgency overrides discernment. A position is vacant. Ministry demands are increasing. Volunteers are exhausted. Momentum feels fragile. In this environment, the primary question quietly shifts from "Is this person aligned and ready?" to "Can someone fill the gap right now?" When pressure governs hiring, authority is entrusted prematurely and without protection.

Pressure hires are rarely reckless. They feel responsible. Leaders convince themselves that action is better than delay, that something is better than nothing, and that problems can be addressed later. This logic is understandable, but it is flawed. Authority granted under pressure is difficult to correct once momentum resumes.

Urgency distorts judgment. Warning signs are minimized. Hard questions are postponed. Concerns are reframed as minor or temporary. Leaders tell themselves that alignment will develop with time or that support structures can compensate for gaps. In practice, misalignment rarely resolves itself once authority has been delegated.

Pressure hires also create moral leverage. Once someone is hired to relieve strain, correcting or removing them later feels ungrateful or destabilizing. Leaders hesitate to address issues because they remember the relief the hire initially provided. This emotional debt weakens governance and delays necessary action.

Congregants and staff closely observe pressure hires. When someone is elevated quickly and without clear alignment, trust erodes. Others wonder why standards were lowered or processes bypassed. Over time, this creates cynicism toward leadership and skepticism toward future decisions.

Pressure hires often lead to role confusion. Because the hire was made to meet immediate needs, the role is poorly defined. Authority boundaries blur. Expectations shift constantly. The individual is set up to fail, and the church bears the consequences.

Faithful churches resist the myth of urgency. Vacancies, though difficult, are rarely as damaging as misaligned authority. Short-term strain is preferable to long-term instability. Delay can be an act of stewardship when it preserves values and protects trust.

Governance provides alternatives to pressure hiring. Interim solutions, redistributed responsibilities, reduced programming, or temporary external support can relieve strain without compromising authority. These options require humility and patience, but they protect the church from preventable harm.

Pressure hires reveal whether values truly govern decisions or merely adorn them. When urgency is allowed to override alignment, values lose authority. When leaders choose restraint under pressure, their values are visibly reinforced.

Faithful churches understand that pressure is not neutral. It pushes decisions toward convenience rather than conviction. By refusing to hire under pressure, churches demonstrate that authority is entrusted carefully, even when doing so costs comfort or momentum.

Avoiding Conflict

Avoiding conflict is one of the most subtle and destructive dynamics in church hiring and leadership. It often presents as kindness, patience, or unity, but its effect is the opposite. When conflict avoidance governs decision-making, clarity is sacrificed, authority weakens, and unchecked misalignment grows.

Church leaders frequently avoid conflict during hiring because they fear appearing ungracious or divisive. Hard questions feel confrontational. Delays feel discouraging. Saying no feels unloving. As a result, concerns are softened, conversations are shortened, and decisions are made to preserve peace rather than to protect faithfulness.

Conflict avoidance does not eliminate conflict. It postpones it. Issues that could have been addressed calmly during discernment later reappear with greater intensity and at greater cost. What might have been a clarifying conversation becomes a relational fracture. What could have been a respectful decline becomes a painful termination.

Avoiding conflict also distorts discernment. Leaders begin interpreting discomfort as a personal failure rather than a warning signal. They explain away internal hesitation and rely on spiritual language to quiet unease. Phrases about peace, unity, or trust are used to bypass clarity rather than to pursue it honestly.

When conflict is avoided, authority becomes relational rather than governed. Decisions are shaped by who might be disappointed, offended, or upset rather than by values and responsibility. This places emotional pressure on leaders and creates inconsistency that others quickly perceive.

Conflict avoidance is especially damaging after hiring. Leaders hesitate to correct early misalignment because they fear damaging rapport. Over time, silence communicates permission. When the correction finally occurs, it feels abrupt and unfair because expectations were never enforced. Trust erodes on both sides.

Scripture does not treat conflict as failure. It treats it as a reality that must be handled with truth and love. Faithfulness requires speaking clearly even when it is uncomfortable. Unity that depends on silence is fragile. Unity grounded in truth is durable.

Faithful churches reframe conflict. They see it not as something to be avoided, but as something to be stewarded. Clear conversations, early boundaries, and honest decisions prevent far greater harm later. Conflict handled early and respectfully strengthens trust rather than weakening it.

Avoiding conflict often feels like mercy. In practice, avoiding conflict is neglect. It leaves people unclear, roles unstable, and authority compromised. Addressing conflict directly, with humility and clarity, is an act of care for both the individual and the church.

When churches stop avoiding conflict and start governing it, hiring decisions become clearer, corrections become fairer, and leadership becomes steadier. Peace is no longer maintained by silence, but by alignment.

Chapter 18 Repairing Damage and Rebuilding Trust

When hiring goes wrong, damage does not remain confined to leadership teams or staff relationships. It ripples outward into congregational trust, volunteer morale, and the church's public witness. Repairing that damage requires more than replacing a person or issuing a statement. It requires intentional rebuilding of trust through clarity, humility, and consistent action over time.

The first step in repair is acknowledgment. Churches often rush past failure to restore normalcy. This instinct misunderstands trust. Trust is not restored by silence or speed. It is restored by honesty. Leaders must name what went wrong at an appropriate level, without defensiveness or oversharing. Acknowledgment signals that values govern authority even when outcomes are uncomfortable.

Ownership must follow acknowledgment. Repairing trust requires leaders to take responsibility for the decision-making process, rather than assigning blame to individuals or circumstances. This does not require public self-flagellation, but it does require humility. When leaders own their role in the failure, credibility is strengthened rather than weakened.

Clarity is essential in rebuilding. Congregants and staff need to understand what will change going forward. Vague assurances that things will get better are insufficient. Trust grows when people see concrete improvements in processes, oversight, and governance. Changes must be visible and sustained, not merely promised.

Time plays a critical role. Trust cannot be expedited. Attempts to accelerate healing often feel manipulative or dismissive. Faithful leaders allow space for questions, grief, and skepticism. They resist the urge to demand confidence before it has been earned.

Consistent enforcement of values is the most powerful trust-building action. People watch what is tolerated after a failure. When standards are enforced evenly and early, confidence slowly returns. When exceptions continue, trust deteriorates further.

Repair also requires care for those directly affected. Staff members, volunteers, and congregants may carry disappointment, confusion, or hurt. Pastoral presence, listening, and appropriate support demonstrate that people matter more than reputation or momentum.

Communication must be measured and truthful. Oversharing creates new harm. Silence breeds speculation. Leaders must strike a careful balance, providing enough information to sustain trust without violating confidentiality or dignity.

Rebuilding trust also involves internal reflection. Churches must capture lessons learned and integrate them into future practice. Failure becomes instructive only when it produces change. Ignoring lessons guarantees repetition.

Finally, leaders must model patience. Rebuilding trust is slow work. It cannot be forced or demanded. Faithful leadership remains steady, transparent, and consistent even when affirmation is delayed.

Repairing damage after hiring failure is difficult, but it is not optional. How a church responds to misalignment reveals its true commitments. When leaders act with humility, clarity, and discipline, trust can be rebuilt. Over time, the church's witness is strengthened not by perfection, but by integrity displayed under pressure.

What To Do After A Failed Hire

A failed hire is not the end of faithful leadership, but it is a defining moment. How a church responds after misalignment becomes clear will either compound the damage or begin the work of restoration. The goal after a failed hire is not damage control. It is integrity.

The first responsibility is to stop the drift. Once it is evident that a hire is misaligned, leaders must act decisively to prevent further harm. This may involve limiting authority, clarifying boundaries, or initiating corrective processes. Delay increases cost. Allowing misalignment to continue in the name of patience or hope is not faithfulness.

Second, leaders must honestly assess the nature of the failure. Not all failed hires are the same. Some involve character issues. Others involve role misfit, unclear authority, or inadequate onboarding. Understanding why the hire failed matters more than how quickly it is resolved. Without this clarity, the same mistakes will be repeated.

Third, leadership must engage correction with transparency and restraint. The individual involved should receive clear communication about concerns, expectations, and next steps. Ambiguity at this stage increases anxiety and resentment. Even difficult conversations can be handled with dignity when clarity and respect are maintained.

Fourth, leaders must decide whether alignment is possible. Some misalignments can be corrected through supervision, role adjustment, or support. Others cannot. When repeated correction does not produce change, leaders must be willing to move toward termination without guilt or delay. Prolonging an unhealthy arrangement does not honor anyone involved.

Fifth, care must be extended appropriately. Failed hires often involve disappointment and loss. Providing pastoral support, referrals, or transition assistance reflects compassion without compromising governance. Care and clarity can coexist.

Sixth, communication must be governed carefully. Leaders should communicate enough to preserve trust without violating confidentiality. Honest acknowledgment of change, coupled with visible commitment to values, reassures the congregation that authority is being stewarded responsibly.

Seventh, leaders must reflect and adjust processes. A failed hire should produce concrete improvements in discernment, onboarding, oversight, or governance. If no changes follow, the failure becomes precedent rather than instruction.

Finally, leaders must model patience and steadiness. Rebuilding trust after a failed hire takes time. Faithful leadership does not demand immediate confidence or praise. It remains consistent, transparent, and values-driven until trust is rebuilt naturally.

A failed hire is painful, but it can be redemptive when handled faithfully. When leaders respond with clarity, courage, and humility, failure becomes a teacher rather than a threat. The church's integrity is preserved not by avoiding mistakes, but by stewarding authority responsibly when mistakes occur.

Communicating With The Congregation

Communication after a hiring failure is one of the most delicate responsibilities leaders face. Done poorly, it deepens mistrust and fuels speculation. Done well, it stabilizes the church and reinforces confidence that values truly govern authority. The goal of congregational communication is not image management. It is trust preservation.

The first principle is restraint. Not everything that leaders know should be shared publicly. Employment matters involve dignity, privacy, and legal responsibility. Oversharing creates new harm and often invites judgment rather than understanding. Faithful communication provides clarity without disclosure that violates trust.

At the same time, silence is not neutral. When leaders say nothing, congregants fill the gaps with assumptions. Rumors grow. Confidence erodes. Communication must acknowledge reality without explaining every detail. Naming that a change has occurred, that leadership has acted, and that values guided the decision reassures the body that authority is being exercised responsibly.

Tone matters as much as content. Communication should be calm, measured, and humble. Defensive explanations or spiritualized language that avoids responsibility undermine credibility. Statements should reflect seriousness, care, and clarity rather than urgency or justification.

Leaders should take ownership of the process without assigning blame. Congregations do not need to know every misstep, but they do need to know that leadership is willing to acknowledge error and correct course. Ownership strengthens trust. Deflection weakens it.

Consistency is essential. What is communicated publicly should align with what is practiced privately. If values are cited, they must be enforced. If processes are referenced, they must exist. Congregants are perceptive. They notice when language and action diverge.

Timing also matters. Communication should not be rushed in response to pressure or delayed to avoid discomfort. Leaders should speak once clarity has been established and the next steps are defined. Premature communication creates confusion. Delayed communication creates suspicion.

Questions and emotions should be expected. Some congregants will feel disappointed, confused, or concerned. Leaders should allow space for appropriate dialogue without opening forums that compromise confidentiality, pastoral presence, and listening matters during these seasons.

Future orientation is important, but it must be grounded in action. Promising to do better is insufficient. Communicating specific changes to process, oversight, or governance demonstrates that lessons have been learned. Trust grows when people see adjustment rather than assurance alone.

Above all, communication should reflect the church's theology of authority. Leaders serve as stewards, not owners. Decisions are made to protect doctrine, culture, and people, not to preserve comfort or reputation. When congregants see leaders act and speak from this posture, confidence returns gradually and authentically.

Faithful communication does not eliminate pain, but it prevents confusion from becoming division. When leaders speak with clarity, restraint, and humility, the congregation is reminded that even in difficulty, values govern authority, and integrity remains intact.

Resetting Governance

When hiring fails, governance must be reset, not merely repaired. Replacing a person without addressing the structures that allowed misalignment guarantees repetition. Resetting governance is the work of reestablishing authority, clarity, and accountability where they weakened or disappeared. It is not an admission of incompetence. It is an act of leadership maturity.

Resetting governance begins with an honest diagnosis. Leaders must examine where authority broke down, not just where behavior failed. This includes asking whether values were clearly defined, whether roles were governed or assumed, whether oversight was active or passive, and whether correction pathways existed and were used. Governance failures are often systemic, not personal.

Authority must be reasserted explicitly. After a failed hire, churches often operate cautiously, avoiding clarity out of fear of further conflict. This hesitation allows informal authority to fill the vacuum. Resetting governance requires naming who holds decision-making authority, how it is exercised, and how accountability functions. Ambiguity after failure compounds damage.

Processes must be formalized where they were previously informal. Discernment steps, hiring approvals, onboarding procedures, supervision rhythms, and correction pathways should be reviewed and documented. Governance that exists only in memory or good intentions is fragile. Governance that is written, shared, and enforced is durable.

Values must be elevated from language to standard. Failed hires often reveal that values were affirmed verbally but not enforced practically. Resetting governance requires leaders to decide what is truly non-negotiable and to apply those standards consistently, even when doing so is uncomfortable. Values regain authority only when they are enforced.

Shared oversight should be strengthened. Concentrated authority increases risk, especially after failure. Resetting governance may require expanding participation in decision-making, clarifying board or elder involvement, or adjusting approval thresholds. This is not about diluting leadership. It is about protecting it.

Communication plays a role both internally and externally. Staff and leaders need clarity about what has changed, why it has changed, and how decisions will be made going forward. Unspoken resets create confusion. Explicit resets create stability.

Resetting governance also requires patience. Trust does not return immediately. Leaders must consistently apply the renewed structure over time without reverting to old habits under pressure. Consistency, not urgency, rebuilds credibility.

Finally, governance must be protected going forward. Churches should resist the temptation to relax structure once stability returns. Pressure will come again. Vacancies will reappear. Growth will create new demands. Governance must remain visible and active, not situational.

Resetting governance is not about control. It is about stewardship. It ensures that authority is exercised responsibly, that people are consistently protected, and that decisions are made according to conviction rather than convenience.

When governance is reset after failure, the church is strengthened rather than diminished. Misalignment becomes instruction. Authority is clarified rather than questioned. Over time, the church's witness is restored not because mistakes were avoided, but because leadership responded with clarity, humility, and disciplined resolve.

APPENDICES

The appendices in this guide are not supplemental reading. They are governing tools. Each appendix is designed to translate conviction into practice and to move hiring from intention to authority.

These materials exist to be used, adopted, and enforced. They are written to stand on their own, but they function best when applied together as a disciplined system. When used selectively or informally, their protective power is weakened. When used consistently, they establish clarity, restraint, and accountability before authority is entrusted.

The appendices provide practical instruments for leaders who recognize that hiring is not merely a staffing decision, but a governance act with doctrinal, cultural, and relational consequences. They are intended to support pastors, elders, boards, and leadership teams who desire to steward authority faithfully rather than reactively.

Each appendix addresses a specific vulnerability commonly found in hiring. Together, they form a framework that clarifies who may hire, how roles are defined, how alignment is assessed, how authority is monitored, and how correction is applied when necessary. These tools are designed to prevent avoidable harm, protect trust, and preserve institutional witness over time.

Churches and organizations are encouraged to adapt these appendices to their polity and context while preserving their governing intent. Language may be contextualized, but authority must not be diluted. Adoption should be formal, not assumed. Use should be disciplined, not occasional.

This appendix provides illustrative examples only and does not replace the step-by-step authority required in the *Pastoral Search Field Manual* or the *Manager Search Field Manual*.

To move forward in a governed and authoritative manner, organizations must employ the recommended field manual for their context:

The Field Manual provides a structured, step-by-step process with defined actions, required questions, documentation expectations, and stop conditions. These manuals exist to ensure that authority is clarified before candidates are considered, values govern decision-making, and both the organization and the leader being entrusted are protected.

When these tools are employed faithfully, hiring becomes an act of stewardship rather than urgency, clarity replaces assumption, and authority is entrusted with confidence rather than hope. The health of the church and the integrity of leadership more broadly are too important to leave hiring unguided.

Appendix A Church Hiring Policy Template

1. Purpose and Authority

1.1 This policy governs all hiring decisions within the church. Hiring is a delegated act of authority that directly affects doctrine, culture, witness, and trust.

1.2 All hiring decisions must align with the church's stated values, doctrinal commitments, and governance structure.

1.3 No position, paid or unpaid, is exempt from this policy where authority, teaching, influence, or discipline is involved.

2. Scope of Application

2.1 This policy applies to all paid staff positions.

2.2 This policy applies to all contracted ministry roles.

2.3 This policy applies to all volunteer roles involving teaching, leadership, pastoral care, or discipline.

2.4 Purely logistical or short-term service roles may follow abbreviated procedures as approved by leadership.

3. Governing Values Requirement

3.1 All hiring decisions must be evaluated against the church's governing values.

3.2 Values function as enforceable standards, not aspirational language.

3.3 Candidates are evaluated against the values. Values are not adjusted to fit candidates.

3.4 No hire may proceed if values alignment is unclear or unresolved.

4. Hiring Authority and Approval

4.1 Hiring authority is delegated as follows.

4.2 Final hiring authority rests with: ____________________

4.3 Required approvals for staff roles include: ____________________

4.4 Roles involving teaching, leadership, or discipline require additional approval by: ____________________

4.5 No individual may unilaterally hire into roles carrying spiritual or organizational authority.

5. Role Definition and Documentation

5.1 A written role description defining authority, responsibility, accountability, and boundaries must be completed before initiating a search.

5.2 A clear statement of reporting structure and supervision must be documented.

5.3 Explicit "This Role Does Not Include" language must be included.

5.4 Employment classification as employee, contractor, or volunteer must be defined.

5.5 Roles may not be filled until all documentation is complete and approved.

6. Discernment and Interview Process

6.1 All candidates must participate in a structured discernment process.

6.2 The discernment process must include multiple interview stages.

6.3 Values-based and situational questioning must be used.

6.4 Doctrinal alignment review must be conducted where applicable.

6.5 Reference and background review appropriate to the role must be completed.

6.6 Hiring decisions may not be based solely on chemistry, gifting, or urgency.

7. References and Background Review

7.1 References must include individuals who have observed the candidate under authority and in conflict.

7.2 General or character-only references are insufficient.

7.3 Background review must be conducted in accordance with legal and ethical standards.

7.4 Background review requirements must be disclosed to candidates in advance.

8. Employment Terms and Compensation

8.1 Compensation and benefits must align with role authority, and responsibility.

8.2 Expectations may not exceed what is reasonably supported by compensation.

8.3 Faith language may not be used to obscure compensation imbalance, role creep, or unclear expectations.

8.4 Bi-vocational roles must be explicitly defined as such.

8.5 Availability expectations and limits must be clearly documented for bi-vocational roles.

9. Onboarding and Oversight

9.1 All new hires must complete a formal onboarding process.

9.2 Onboarding must include a review of values, authority, and accountability.

9.3 Supervision and mentoring relationships must be clarified.

9.4 Expectations and evaluation rhythms must be documented.

9.5 Oversight is required throughout the first year and beyond.

10. Correction, Discipline, and Restoration

10.1 The church affirms correction and discipline as acts of stewardship.

10.2 Processes for correction must be clear, documented, and proportionate.

10.3 Correction and discipline must be governed by values rather than emotion or urgency.

10.4 Restoration does not imply reinstatement to role or authority.

11. Termination and Transition

11.1 Termination may occur when alignment cannot be restored.

11.2 Termination decisions must follow documented processes.

11.3 Termination must be handled with dignity, restraint, and care.

11.4 Congregational communication must protect privacy while preserving trust.

12. Policy Review and Enforcement

12.1 This policy must be reviewed every ________________ years or following significant staffing changes.

12.2 Failure to follow this policy invalidates hiring authority and requires corrective review.

13. Adoption

13.1 This policy was reviewed and adopted by the appropriate governing body of the church.

13.2 Date of adoption: ________________

13.3 Approving authority: ________________

13.4 Signature: ________________

Appendix B: Role Definition and Authority Map

This appendix provides a structured framework for defining roles, authority, and accountability before hiring or assigning responsibility. It is designed to prevent ambiguity, overreach, and underperformance by making authority explicit rather than assumed.

This tool should be completed before any role is posted, filled, or reassigned.

1. Purpose of the Role Definition and Authority Map

1.1 The purpose of this map is to clarify how authority is distributed, exercised, and overseen within each role.

1.2 The map ensures that responsibility, authority, and accountability remain aligned.

1.3 No role should be filled without completing this map where influence, teaching, leadership, or decision-making authority is involved.

2. Role Identification

2.1 Role title: ______________________________

2.2 Ministry or department: ______________________________

2.3 Employment classification
Employee ☐
Contractor ☐
Volunteer ☐
Bi-vocational ☐

2.4 Full-time ☐ Part-time ☐ Hours per week: ___________

3. Core Function of the Role

3.1 The primary purpose of this role is:

3.2 The core responsibilities of this role include:

3.3 The outcomes this role is responsible for stewarding (not merely producing) are:

---

4. Authority Granted to the Role

4.1 This role has the authority to make decisions in the following areas:

4.2 This role has the authority to lead or direct the following people or teams:

4.3 This role has authority to represent the church publicly or internally in the following ways:

4.4 This role includes teaching, spiritual instruction, or doctrinal influence.
Yes ☐ No ☐

If yes, specify scope:

---

5. Authority Explicitly Withheld From the Role

5.1 This role does not have authority in the following areas:

5.2 This role does not have the authority to discipline, correct, or remove others unless explicitly delegated.
Yes ☐ No ☐

5.3 This role does not have the authority to commit the church financially beyond approved limits.
Yes ☐ No ☐

5.4 Additional "This Role Does Not Include" clarifications:

---

6. Accountability and Oversight

6.1 This role reports directly to: ______________________________

6.2 Oversight authority rests with: ______________________________

6.3 Evaluation of this role will be conducted by:

____

6.4 Frequency of formal evaluation:
Monthly ☐ Quarterly ☐ Annually ☐

6.5 Documentation of evaluation and correction is required.
Yes ☐ No ☐

7. Decision Escalation Path

7.1 Decisions that must be escalated to a higher authority include:

7.2 Situations requiring consultation before action include:

7.3 Final decision authority in disputed matters rests with:

---

8. Values and Doctrinal Guardrails

8.1 The governing values this role is expected to enforce and protect include:

8.2 The doctrinal commitments this role must affirm and operate within include:

8.3 Misalignment with values or doctrine triggers the corrective process under policy.
Yes ☐ No ☐

9. Role Risk Assessment

9.1 This role carries elevated risk due to influence, visibility, or authority.
Yes ☐ No ☐

9.2 Identified risks associated with this role include:

9.3 Safeguards required to protect the church and the role holder include:

---

10. Approval and Adoption

10.1 This Role Definition and Authority Map has been reviewed and approved.

10.2 Reviewed by: ______________________________

10.3 Date: ______________________________

10.4 Signature: ______________________________

This appendix exists to make authority visible before it is entrusted. When roles are clearly defined, accountability is fair, corrections are possible, and trust is preserved.

Appendix C: Values Alignment Assessment

This appendix provides a disciplined tool for evaluating values alignment before authority is entrusted. It is designed to move values from stated agreement to observable alignment. This assessment should be completed during the discernment process and revisited during onboarding and the first year of oversight.

Values alignment is not assumed. It is evaluated.

1. Purpose of the Values Alignment Assessment

1.1 The purpose of this assessment is to determine whether a candidate's convictions, patterns, and posture align with the church's governing values.

1.2 This assessment prioritizes lived alignment over verbal affirmation.

1.3 Completion of this assessment is required for all roles involving authority, teaching, influence, or leadership.

2. Governing Values Identification

2.1 List the church's governing values relevant to this role.

Value 1: ____

Value 2: ____

Value 3: ____

Value 4: ____

2.2 These values function as enforceable standards, not aspirational language.
Confirmed ☐

3. Candidate Self-Assessment

3.1 Candidate affirms understanding of the governing values.
Yes ☐ No ☐

3.2 Candidate describes how these values shape their decisions and behavior.
Summary: ____

3.3 Candidate identifies which value they find most challenging and why.
Response: ____

3.4 Candidate describes a situation where a value cost them something personally or professionally.
Response: ____

4. Behavioral Evidence Review

4.1 Evidence of consistent alignment with Value 1:
Observed pattern: ________________________________

4.2 Evidence of consistent alignment with Value 2:
Observed pattern: ________________________________

4.3 Evidence of consistent alignment with Value 3:
Observed pattern: ________________________________

4.4 Evidence of consistent alignment with Value 4:
Observed pattern: ________________________________

4.5 Areas where alignment is unclear or untested:

____

5. Authority and Values Under Pressure

5.1 Candidate describes how they respond when values conflict with outcomes or expectations.
Response: ____

5.2 Candidate describes how they respond to corrections related to values.
Response: ____

5.3 Candidate demonstrates willingness to submit to values enforcement.
Yes ☐ No ☐

6. Values Versus Preferences

6.1 Areas where candidate preferences differ from governing values:

6.2 Candidate acknowledges distinction between personal preference and values authority.
Yes ☐ No ☐

6.3 Any preference conflicts requiring clarification before hiring:

---

7. Cultural and Relational Alignment

7.1 Candidate demonstrates alignment with the church's relational culture without requiring uniformity.
Yes ☐ No ☐

7.2 Areas of cultural tension identified:

7.3 Safeguards required to protect values without cloning personality:

____

8. Risk Indicators Related to Values

8.1 Evidence of defensiveness when values are discussed.
Yes ☐ No ☐

8.2 Evidence of ambiguity or avoidance in values-related responses.
Yes ☐ No ☐

8.3 History of conflict related to values enforcement.
Yes ☐ No ☐

If yes, explanation: ________________________________

9. Alignment Determination

9.1 Overall values alignment assessment:
Aligned ☐ Conditionally Aligned ☐ Not Aligned ☐

9.2 Conditions required for alignment if conditional:

____

9.3 Recommendation regarding entrusting authority at this time:
Proceed ☐ Delay ☐ Do Not Proceed ☐

10. Review and Approval

10.1 This Values Alignment Assessment has been reviewed by appropriate leadership.

10.2 Reviewed by: ________________________________

10.3 Date: ________________________________

10.4 Signature: ______________________________

This assessment exists to protect the church from assuming alignment where none exists and to protect candidates from being entrusted with authority they are not prepared to steward. When values are clearly evaluated and consistently enforced, hiring becomes an act of faithful governance rather than a hopeful intention.

Appendix D: Doctrinal Agreement Statement

This appendix provides a formal mechanism for affirming doctrinal alignment before authority is entrusted. It is not designed to test theological sophistication or demand uniformity on secondary matters. It exists to clarify essential beliefs, teaching boundaries, and accountability related to doctrine.

Doctrinal agreement is a condition of authority, not merely of membership.

1. Purpose of the Doctrinal Agreement Statement

1.1 The purpose of this statement is to confirm alignment with the church's essential doctrinal commitments before a role involving teaching, leadership, or spiritual influence is assumed.

1.2 This statement distinguishes between essential doctrine, secondary theological matters, and personal conviction.

1.3 Completion of this statement is required for all roles involving teaching, preaching, discipleship, pastoral care, or doctrinal influence.

2. Scope of Doctrinal Authority

2.1 This agreement applies to roles with authority to teach, interpret Scripture publicly, lead spiritually, or influence doctrinal understanding.

2.2 Roles without teaching or doctrinal authority may follow an abbreviated affirmation as determined by leadership.

2.3 Doctrinal agreement does not grant teaching authority. It confirms eligibility for it.

3. **Essential Doctrinal Affirmation**

3.1 The candidate affirms agreement with the church's essential doctrinal statement as adopted by the governing body.
Yes ☐ No ☐

3.2 The essential doctrines affirmed include, but are not limited to:

3.3 The candidate understands that these doctrines are non-negotiable within teaching, leadership, and public representation.
Yes ☐ No ☐

4. **Teaching and Representation Boundaries**

4.1 The candidate agrees to teach and represent doctrine within the boundaries of the church's affirmed beliefs.
Yes ☐ No ☐

4.2 The candidate agrees not to promote alternative doctrines, interpretations, or theological positions that contradict essential beliefs while serving in this role.
Yes ☐ No ☐

4.3 The candidate agrees to seek clarification or permission before addressing disputed or sensitive theological topics publicly.
Yes ☐ No ☐

5. **Secondary Matters and Personal Convictions**

5.1 The candidate acknowledges that differences may exist on secondary theological matters.
Yes ☐ No ☐

5.2 The candidate agrees not to elevate secondary matters to divisive or authoritative teaching positions.
Yes ☐ No ☐

5.3 Any known areas of theological difference are disclosed below:

5.4 Leadership has reviewed these differences and determined they are acceptable within the scope of the role.
Yes ☐ No ☐

6. Accountability and Correction

6.1 The candidate agrees to submit to doctrinal oversight and correction by the appropriate authority.
Yes ☐ No ☐

6.2 The candidate understands that doctrinal misalignment may result in correction, limitation of authority, or removal from the role.
Yes ☐ No ☐

6.3 Doctrinal correction will be governed by documented processes and applied with clarity and restraint.
Acknowledged ☐

7. Public and Digital Representation

7.1 The candidate understands that public teaching, published material, and digital communication are forms of doctrinal representation.
Yes ☐ No ☐

7.2 The candidate agrees to represent the church's doctrine faithfully in public and online contexts related to their role.
Yes ☐ No ☐

8. Term and Review of Agreement

8.1 This doctrinal agreement applies for the duration of the role and is subject to review if doctrine, role scope, or governance changes.

8.2 Renewal or reaffirmation may be required periodically as determined by leadership.

9. Affirmation and Signature

9.1 I affirm that I have reviewed and understand the church's doctrinal commitments and agree to operate within them as outlined above.

Name: ____

Signature: ___________________________________

Date: ____

10. Leadership Review and Acceptance

10.1 This Doctrinal Agreement Statement has been reviewed and accepted by appropriate leadership.

Reviewed by: _________________________________

Date: _______________________________________

Signature: ___________________________________

This statement exists to protect doctrine, preserve unity, and clarify teaching authority. When doctrinal agreement is explicit and governed, churches avoid confusion, prevent drift, and steward spiritual authority with integrity rather than assumption.

Appendix E: Interview Question Bank

This appendix provides a structured set of interview questions designed to surface values alignment, authority posture, doctrinal clarity, and readiness for responsibility. These questions are not intended to be used all at once. They should be selected and sequenced according to role authority, interview stage, and discernment needs.

Questions should be asked consistently across candidates and evaluated collectively.

1. Purpose of the Interview Question Bank

1.1 The purpose of this question bank is to move interviews beyond chemistry, gifting, and résumé review into disciplined discernment.

1.2 These questions are designed to reveal patterns of behavior, posture under authority, and alignment with governing values.

1.3 This question bank supports, but does not replace, prayer, wisdom, and shared discernment.

2. Core Values Alignment Questions

2.1 Which of our stated values most shapes how you make decisions, and why?

2.2 Describe a situation where living out a core value cost you something personally or professionally.

2.3 Tell us about a time when a value you held conflicted with expected outcomes. How did you respond?

2.4 Which value do you find most difficult to live out consistently, and what safeguards do you rely on?

3. Authority and Accountability Questions

3.1 Describe a time when your decision was overruled by leadership. How did you respond?

3.2 Tell us about a situation where you were corrected. What was your initial reaction, and what changed afterward?

3.3 How do you distinguish between healthy submission and unhealthy compliance?

3.4 What expectations do you have of those who supervise you?

4. Behavioral and Situational Questions

4.1 Describe a conflict you did not handle well. What did you learn from it?

4.2 Tell us about a time when you had to enforce a boundary that was unpopular.

4.3 Describe a situation where you had to say no to someone you cared about for the sake of responsibility or integrity.

4.4 How do you respond when expectations are unclear or change unexpectedly?

5. Doctrine and Teaching Questions

(Use only for roles involving teaching, leadership, or spiritual instruction.)

5.1 Which doctrines do you consider essential, and why?

5.2 Describe a theological position you hold strongly. How do you handle disagreement on that issue?

5.3 Tell us about a time when you chose not to teach or share a conviction because it was not appropriate for your role or context.

5.4 How do you discern what should be taught publicly versus discussed privately?

6. Character and Integrity Questions

6.1 Describe a situation where no one would have known if you chose the easier path. What did you do?

6.2 How do you guard against misuse of influence or authority?

6.3 Tell us about a failure that required humility to address.

6.4 What practices help you remain accountable in private life?

7. Relational and Cultural Alignment Questions

7.1 Describe the healthiest team culture you have been part of. What made it healthy?

7.2 What type of culture is most challenging for you to work within, and why?

7.3 How do you handle working with people whose style or personality differs significantly from yours?

7.4 What behaviors from leadership help you do your best work?

8. Pressure and Discernment Questions

8.1 Describe a season when you felt pressured to act quickly. How did you maintain clarity?

8.2 How do you recognize when urgency is affecting your judgment?

8.3 Tell us about a time when waiting was the harder but wiser choice.

9. Red Flag and Clarification Questions

(Use selectively when ambiguity, defensiveness, or avoidance appears.)

9.1 Can you help us understand that answer more specifically?

9.2 What would someone who disagrees with you say about that situation?

9.3 Is there any part of your history that might raise concern for us in this role?

9.4 What questions were you hoping we would not ask?

10. Closing and Discernment Questions

10.1 What concerns do you have about this role that we have not discussed?

10.2 What boundaries would you need in place to serve faithfully and sustainably?

10.3 What would misalignment look like to you in the first year?

10.4 What would help you receive correction well in this role?

11. Interviewer Reflection Questions

(To be completed by leadership after interviews.)

11.1 Did the candidate demonstrate clarity or ambiguity when discussing values and authority?

11.2 Did the candidate respond to pressure with defensiveness or reflection?

11.3 Were patterns consistent across answers, references, and behavior?

11.4 Is alignment confirmed, or are we hoping it **will develop later?**

12. **Use** and Governance of This Question Bank

12.1 Questions should be documented and responses summarized.

12.2 No single answer should determine a decision. Patterns matter.

12.3 Discomfort during questioning is not disqualifying. Avoidance and defensiveness may be.

12.4 Hiring decisions should be delayed when clarity is incomplete.

This question bank exists to discipline discernment. When questions are intentional, shared, and governed, interviews become acts of stewardship rather than persuasion. Authority is entrusted carefully, and alignment is confirmed before responsibility is assigned.

Appendix F: Reference Check Guide

This appendix provides a disciplined framework for conducting reference checks that confirm alignment rather than merely affirming reputation. References are not endorsements. They are verification tools designed to reveal patterns of behavior, posture under authority, and readiness for entrusted responsibility.

This guide should be used after interviews and before authority is formally granted.

1. Purpose of the Reference Check Guide

1.1 The purpose of reference checks is to confirm what has been observed during interviews and discernment, not to discover alignment for the first time.

1.2 Reference checks exist to surface patterns that candidates may not disclose, and interviews cannot fully reveal.

1.3 Reference checks are required for all roles involving authority, teaching, leadership, pastoral care, or public representation.

2. Selecting Appropriate References

2.1 References should include individuals who have directly supervised the candidate.

2.2 References should include individuals who have observed the candidate under authority and in conflict.

2.3 Peer-only or character-only references are insufficient on their own.

2.4 At least one reference should be outside the candidate's current organization when possible.

2.5 References with close personal or family relationships to the candidate should be noted and weighed carefully.

3. Preparing for the Reference Conversation

3.1 Reference conversations should be scheduled, not rushed.

3.2 References should be informed that the conversation is confidential and governance-related.

3.3 Interviewers should review interview notes and identify areas of concern before the call.

3.4 Questions should be asked consistently across references.

4. Core Reference Questions

4.1 How long have you known the candidate, and in what capacity?

4.2 In what areas did the candidate carry authority or responsibility?

4.3 How did the candidate respond to correction or disagreement?

4.4 Can you describe a conflict involving the candidate and how it was handled?

4.5 What boundaries did the candidate respect well, and where were boundaries tested?

4.6 How did the candidate handle pressure, disappointment, or unmet expectations?

5. Values and Character Questions

5.1 Which of the candidate's values were most visible in daily practice?

5.2 Were there values the candidate struggled to live out consistently?

5.3 How did the candidate handle situations where integrity was costly?

5.4 Did you ever have to address issues of honesty, humility, or accountability?

6. Authority and Trust Questions

6.1 How did the candidate exercise authority over others?

6.2 Did the candidate ever overstep authority or resist oversight?

6.3 Would you trust this candidate with greater responsibility? Why or why not?

6.4 Are there roles or contexts where you would hesitate to place this candidate?

7. Performance Versus Posture

7.1 How effective was the candidate in producing results?

7.2 How did effectiveness affect the candidate's humility and teachability?

7.3 Were concerns ever minimized because outcomes were positive?

8. Closing Clarification Questions

8.1 What concerns, if any, should we consider seriously before proceeding?

8.2 Is there anything you would want us to know that we have not asked?

8.3 Would you rehire or reappoint this candidate under your authority?

9. Interpreting Reference Responses

9.1 Vague praise without examples should be weighed cautiously.

9.2 Hesitation, guarded language, or overqualification of answers should be noted.

9.3 Patterns across multiple references carry more weight than isolated comments.

9.4 Silence on key areas may indicate avoidance rather than absence of concern.

10. Documentation and Governance

10.1 Reference conversations must be documented with factual summaries, not impressions.

10.2 Documentation should focus on patterns, examples, and consistency.

10.3 Reference findings should be reviewed collectively by those with hiring authority.

10.4 No single reference should determine a decision.

11. Ethical and Legal Guardrails

11.1 References must be conducted in accordance with legal and ethical standards.

11.2 Questions must relate directly to role readiness, authority, and alignment.

11.3 Information obtained must be handled confidentially and shared only with appropriate leadership.

12. Final Reference Assessment

12.1 Reference review outcome:
Confirmed Alignment ☐ Conditional Alignment ☐ Alignment Not Confirmed ☐

12.2 Conditions or concerns requiring clarification:

12.3 Recommendation regarding proceeding with hire:
Proceed ☐ Delay ☐ Do Not Proceed ☐

This guide exists to protect the church from false confidence and to protect candidates from being entrusted with authority based on incomplete information. When references are approached with discipline and interpreted with wisdom, they become safeguards rather than formalities, confirming alignment before responsibility is entrusted.

Appendix G: First-Year Evaluation Framework

This appendix provides a structured framework for evaluating alignment, stewardship, and authority during the first year of service. The first year is not a probationary test of worth. It is an intentional season of confirmation, correction, and clarity. Evaluation during this period protects the church, supports the role holder, and prevents long-term misalignment from becoming entrenched.

This framework should be used for all roles involving authority, teaching, leadership, or public representation.

1. Purpose of the First-Year Evaluation Framework

1.1 The purpose of this framework is to confirm alignment between role definition, values, authority, and lived practice.

1.2 The first year is understood as an installation period, not merely an orientation phase.

1.3 Evaluation during the first year prioritizes faithfulness, posture, and alignment over outcomes alone.

1.4 Completion of this framework is required before authority is considered fully entrusted.

2. Evaluation Rhythm and Timeline

2.1 Formal evaluations should occur at the following intervals.
30 days ☐
90 days ☐
6 months ☐
12 months ☐

2.2 Informal check-ins should occur regularly between formal evaluations.

2.3 Missed evaluations weaken oversight and must be corrected promptly.

3. Role and Authority Confirmation

3.1 The role as written remains accurate and enforceable.
Confirmed ☐ Needs Revision ☐

3.2 Authority granted has been exercised within defined boundaries.
Yes ☐ No ☐

3.3 Any instances of authority confusion or overreach are documented below.

3.4 Any authority gaps or underutilization are documented below.

---

4. Values Alignment Review

4.1 The role holder demonstrates consistent alignment with governing values.
Yes ☐ Partially ☐ No ☐

4.2 Evidence of alignment observed in daily behavior includes:

4.3 Situations where values were tested and how they were handled:

4.4 Areas where values alignment requires correction or reinforcement:

---

5. **Accountability and Posture**

5.1 The role holder responds to correction with humility and clarity.
Yes ☐ No ☐

5.2 The role holder seeks clarity rather than operating independently when uncertain.
Yes ☐ No ☐

5.3 Evidence of teachability and restraint under pressure:

---

6. **Relationships and Team Integration**

6.1 The role holder integrates well within existing leadership structures.
Yes ☐ No ☐

6.2 Conflicts or tensions encountered and how they were addressed:

6.3 Relational boundaries are respected and maintained.
Yes ☐ No ☐

7. **Doctrine and Teaching Oversight**
   (Complete only for roles involving teaching or doctrinal influence.)

7.1 Teaching remains within affirmed doctrinal boundaries.
Yes ☐ No ☐

7.2 Any doctrinal concerns raised and how they were addressed:

7.3 The role holder demonstrates discernment regarding what should and should not be taught publicly.
Yes ☐ No ☐

8. Performance and Stewardship

8.1 Responsibilities are being stewarded faithfully.
Yes ☐ Partially ☐ No ☐

8.2 Outcomes are evaluated in light of values and authority, not results alone.
Confirmed ☐

8.3 Areas of strength observed:

8.4 Areas requiring development or support:

---

9. Correction and Early Intervention

9.1 Corrections have been addressed promptly and clearly.
Yes ☐ No ☐

9.2 Unresolved issues requiring attention:

9.3 Patterns of concern requiring escalation or limitation of authority:

---

10. Determination at One Year

10.1 Alignment with role, values, and authority is confirmed.
Yes ☐ No ☐

10.2 Authority may be fully entrusted going forward.
Yes ☐ With Conditions ☐ No ☐

10.3 Conditions or safeguards required if authority is conditional:

10.4 Recommendation regarding continuation in role:
Continue ☐ Modify Role ☐ Delay Authority ☐ Transition ☐

11. Review and Documentation

11.1 This evaluation has been reviewed by appropriate leadership.

11.2 Reviewed by: ______________________________

11.3 Date: ____________________________________

11.4 Signature: ______________________________

This framework exists to ensure that alignment is confirmed before authority is assumed. When the first year is guided with clarity and care, corrections are timely, trust is protected, and leadership is strengthened. Faithful oversight early prevents painful repair later and allows authority to be entrusted with confidence rather than hope.

www.ingramcontent.com/pod-product-compliance
Lightning Source LLC
LaVergne TN
LVHW090606110826
845146LV00001B/285